AMERICA
AN AERIAL VIEW

PHOTOGRAPHS: **JAMES DOANE**
LAYOUT: J. OPISSO
INTRODUCTION: M. WIESENTHAL

1st. Edition, March 1978
2nd. Edition, June 1979

I.S.B.N.
84-7424-013-1

INTRODUCTION

America, America... mythical country and unknown land of the first navigators. Wheat, wool, coffee, gold, oranges, coal, herds of animals, enormous rivers like the Mississippi and the Missouri; the seas of California and Florida, fir trees, oak, pines, chestnut trees, smooth prairies, frozen plains, eagles and doves, ducks and hawks, red men and black men, yellow and white men.
America, America... the dream of millions of emigrants who cross waters to work in her fields, factories and workshops.
Fifty states and an incredible diversity of races, ideas and religions.
It is only with the imagination of a poet, according to Walt Whitman, that this vast mosaic of nations can be understood. With the imagination of a poet, or the wings of an eagle. Perhaps with both things at the same time like Jim Doane, the photographer who produced the magnificent photographs in this book, who has flown over the lands of Florida and Alaska, California and the Grand Canyon.
America, America... the country of the future for our grand-parents, today counts and celebrates its past in centenaries. Let's explore it, in all directions, from coast to coast, from frontier to frontier, flying through the sky. Let's view this land from the air, to see its light and shadows, feel its breath, its movement, its silence and its life.
America, America...

Jim Doane, the author of these photographs, works as a Captain for Eastern Airlines. Raised in Canton (Ohio) and educated at the Ohio State University, thanks to his profession as a pilot, he has had the opportunity to travel the length and breadth of the United States and capture the most unusual aspects of its geographical features. This book and the series of magnificent photographs illustrating it is the fruit of his experience as a pilot and photographer.

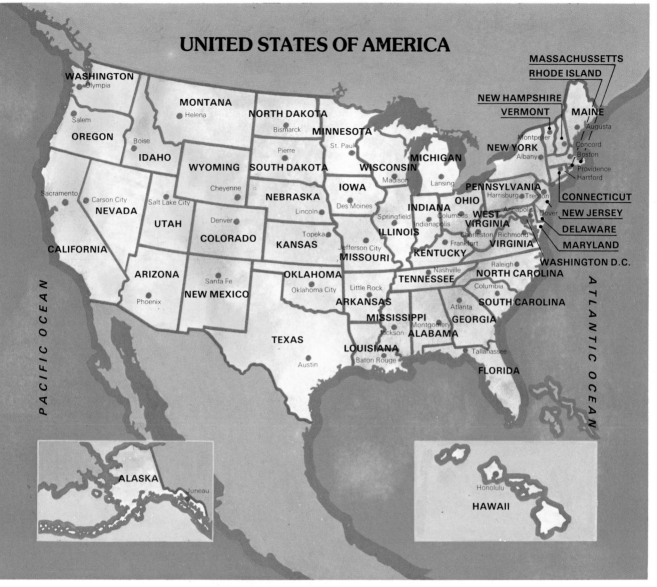

UNITED STATES OF AMERICA

WASHINGTON
Olympia

Salem

OREGON

Boise

IDAHO

Sacramento

Carson City

NEVADA

CALIFORNIA

UTAH

Salt Lake City

ARIZONA

Phoenix

NEW MEXICO

Santa Fe

MONTANA

Helena

NORTH DAKOTA

Bismarck

MINNESOTA

Pierre

St. Paul

WYOMING

SOUTH DAKOTA

WISCONSIN

Madison

Cheyenne

IOWA

NEBRASKA

Lincoln

Des Moines

Denver

COLORADO

Topeka

KANSAS

Jefferson City

MISSOURI

OKLAHOMA

Oklahoma City

Little Rock

ARKANSAS

TEXAS

Austin

LOUISIANA

Baton Rouge

MICHIGAN

Lansing

MASSACHUSSETTS

RHODE ISLAND

NEW HAMPSHIRE

VERMONT

MAINE

Augusta

Montpelier

Concord

Boston

NEW YORK

Albany

Providence

Hartford

PENNSYLVANIA

Harrisburg

Trenton

CONNECTICUT

OHIO

Columbus

INDIANA

Indianapolis

Annapolis

Dover

NEW JERSEY

WEST VIRGINIA

DELAWARE

Springfield

ILLINOIS

Charleston

Richmond

MARYLAND

Frankfort

VIRGINIA

WASHINGTON D.C.

KENTUCKY

Nashville

Raleigh

NORTH CAROLINA

TENNESSEE

Columbia

SOUTH CAROLINA

MISSISSIPPI

Atlanta

GEORGIA

Montgomery

Jackson

ALABAMA

Tallahassee

FLORIDA

PACIFIC OCEAN

ATLANTIC OCEAN

ALASKA

Juneau

HAWAII

Honolulu

ALPHABETICAL LISTING OF STATES

WASHINGTON, D.C.

CAPITAL OF THE UNITED STATES

ESTABLISHED IN 1791

AREA -67 sq. miles
-174 sq. km.

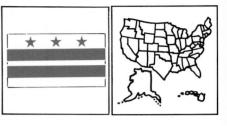

1

Washington, D.C., the capital of the United States, is one of the most beautiful cities in the world.

The "heartbeat" of our country, Washington has a clean, spacious appearance . . . cloaked with a cosmopolitan, yet unhurried atmosphere. The city is designed with more park space than any other city. Rock Creek park alone covers 1,754 acres.

The District of Columbia houses many universities, historical monuments, and educational centers. It is the home of the President of the United States, who resides at 1600 Pennsylvania Avenue in the famous White House. Visiting the "Capital City" is an experience of a lifetime.

THE WHITE HOUSE
The home of every president since John Adams, the White House is surrounded by beautiful lawns and trees. Throughout the corridors and reception rooms are portraits of all the presidents — including the famous Gilbert Stuart portrait of George Washington.

PENTAGON — ARLINGTON, VA.
A city within itself, this 5-sided structure is the world's largest "office building".

JOHN F. KENNEDY GRAVE — ARLINGTON NATIONAL CEMETERY
The grave of John F. Kennedy overlooks the nation's capital from Arlington National Cemetery —burial place of many government and military officials. Around 60,000 war dead are buried here, including the "Unknown Soldier".

THE CAPITOL
Home of the United States Senate and House of Representatives, the Capitol has been used for every presidential inauguration since that of Andrew Jackson. Atop the Capitol stands the huge bronze statue of Freedom.

1. JEFFERSON MEMORIAL,
   WASHINGTON MONUMENT, AND THE WHITE HOUSE.
2. PENTAGON — ARLINGTON, VA.
3. JOHN F. KENNEDY GRAVE — ARLINGTON
   NATIONAL CEMETERY
4. THE CAPITOL

2

3

4

ALABAMA

CAPITAL -
MONTGOMERY

22nd. STATE
DECEMBER 14, 1819

AREA -51,609 sq. miles
-133,667 sq. km.

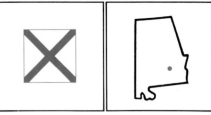

1

Since the Spaniards first poked along the Gulf Coast in 1519, Alabama's rich heritage has included associations with the French, British and Spanish until the Louisiana Purchase. The Creek Indians then claimed title until Andrew Jackson was victorious at Horseshoe Bend. Alabama met statehood requirements in 1819, following a surge of homesteaders.

Formerly noted for cotton, Alabama now offers a diversified list of agricultural and manufacturing products - with steel heading the list.

ALABAMA SPACE AND ROCKET CENTER — TRANQUILITY BASE — HUNTSVILLE

This space center was built by the citizens of Alabama and dedicated to "those Americans who have made it possible for man to walk on the moon and to explore the universe" and to the youth of America who will use the technology of space for the benefit of mankind.

VULCAN

The largest iron figure ever cast, standing 55 feet high and weighing 120,000 pounds. Vulcan overlooks Birmingham, the largest city in Alabama. Named after the Roman god of fire, Vulcan is one of the few monuments in the world to symbolize industry.

MOUNDVILLE STATE PARK — NEAR TUSCALOOSA

Nationally recognized as one of the greatest prehistoric Indian sites in America, Moundville Park was once a thriving ceremonial center of the Mississippi culture. The ruins of 40 large earth mounds encircle an area of over 320 acres bordered by the Black Warrior River.

HORTON MILL COVERED BRIDGE — ONEONTA

Recorded in the national Register, this 220-foot rustic relic is higher than any above-water covered bridge in America.

1. ALABAMA SPACE AND ROCKET CENTER —
   TRANQUILITY BASE — HUNTSVILLE
2. VULCAN — BIRMINGHAM
3. MOUNDVILLE STATE PARK — NEAR TUSCALOOSA
4. HORTON MILL COVERED BRIDGE —
   ONEONTA

2

3

4

ALASKA

CAPITAL - **JUNEAU**

49th. STATE
JANUARY 3, 1959

AREA -586,412 sq. mil.
-1,518,807 sq. km

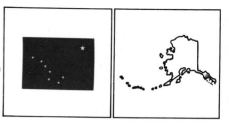

The next to last state to join the union, Alaska is unique in many respects. It is America's most northern state, but also contains the most western area in the United States — Little Diomede Island, which snuggles up to the International Date Line, just 3 miles away from Russia's Big Diomede Island. And part of Alaska is also the most eastern point in the United States. Pochnoi Point, on Semisopochnoi Island in the Aleutians, lies across the 180th meridian, and is in the Eastern Hemisphere.

Alaska is BIG. More than twice the size of Texas... and as large as the next three largest states combined. There are 6 different climatic and geographic areas in Alaska, which is why it is often called "six states within a state". These areas range from the damp rain forests of southeast Alaska . . . to the great delta system of western Alaska . . . to the frozen barrens of Arctic Alaska.

In its 586,400 square miles are tremendous mountain ranges. Many active volcanoes are found in Alaska, as well as some of the world's most extensive glaciers. One of these — the Malaspina — is larger than the entire state of Rhode Island.

Alaska's coastline is 33,904 miles in length — greater than all of the other coastal states combined; and another 560,000 square miles of Alaska are underwater. Beneath the waters of the 2 oceans and 3 seas, which wash Alaska's shores, is 65% of this nation's continental shelf, rich in products of the sea and oil.

ANCHORAGE

Overlooking Cook Inlet from a high bluff, Anchorage is situated at the base of the snow-crested Chugach Range. Half of Alaska's population is located here due to the influence of commerce and industry . . . along with the state's finest rail, air and highway connections.

MT. McKINLEY NATIONAL PARK

Mt. McKinley National Park encompasses 3,030 square miles of towering mountains, alpine glaciers and gently-rolling lowlands crossed by broad rivers. Mt. McKinley, or Denali — "the high one," towers 20,320 feet above the surrounding lowlands, making it America's tallest mountain. The upper two thirds of the mountain are perpetually sheathed in ice and snow, and the glaciers reach up to 30 miles long.

PORTAGE GLACIER

Spectacular million-ton icebergs, spawned by glaciers that descended from gigantic snow-covered mountains, provide once-in-a-lifetime thrills as the thundering fury of the crashing glaciers unfolds before your very eyes. Portage Glacier, bridging a narrow isthmus between Cook Inlet and Prince William Sound, is less than an hour's drive from Anchorage.

3

4

1. ANCHORAGE
2. MT. McKINLEY
   RUTH GLACIER
3. PORTAGE GLACIER
4. KNIK GLACIER

ARIZONA

CAPITAL - **PHOENIX**
48th. STATE
FEBRUARY 14, 1912
AREA -113,909 sq. mil.
-295,024 sq. km.

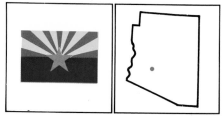

1

2

3

4

Known as the "Grand Canyon State", Arizona houses one of the nation's most famous scenic attractions, the Grand Canyon. Within Arizona's borders are also the Petrified Forest and the Painted Desert. One quarter of the state's land is occupied by a total of 19 Indian reservations — the largest of these belonging to the Navajos.

The history of Arizona can be separated into 3 periods: The Indian supremacy, the Spanish occupation and the American period. By the Treaty of Guadalupe-Hidalgo in 1848 and the Gadsden Purchase in 1853, Arizona became part of the United States. It was admitted to the union in 1912 as the 48th state.

LONDON BRIDGE
Stretching across the Colorado River at Lake Havasu City, the London Bridge was once the famous cross-over on the Thames River in London, England. Transported block by block from England, and re-assembled in its original form, this striking landmark is part of an international airport.

SUNSET CRATER NATIONAL MONUMENT
Dominating the surrounding fields of cinder dunes, lava squeeze-ups, spatter cones and inactive hot springs, stands the deformed cone of the Sunset Crater. Dark at the base, the volcano becomes rosy, then turns to various shades of yellow — giving it the appearance of

being in the constant light of a sunset. It is about 1,300 ft. in diameter and 400 ft. deep. Humphry's Peak, 12,633', in the background offers snow skiing virtually in the middle of the desert.

MONUMENT VALLEY
Monument Valley is noted for its many solitary monoliths of red sandstone that tower as much as 1,000 feet above the valley floor. Strange and gigantic forms, caused by years of erosion, can also be seen within the park. Monument Valley lies within the Navajo Reservation.

LITTLE COLORADO RIVER AND PAINTED DESERT
This vast area of plateaus, buttes and low mesas — —almost devoid of water and plant life — is known for the brilliant colors of its sandstones, shales and clay. The Painted Desert is located in northeast Arizona, extending northeast of the Grand Canyon along the Colorado River, and southeast along the Little Colorado River and the Petrified Forest.

GRAND CANYON
The Grand Canyon is one of the seven wonders of the world. Taking 10 million years, the canyon was formed by the slow rise of the Colorado Plateau. As this land rose, the Colorado River gradually cut the Grand Canyon to a depth of nearly a mile below the South Rim, and to a width of from 4 to 8 miles. Before its discovery by García López de Cardenas in 1540, the Grand Canyon was the home of many Indian tribes.

1. LONDON BRIDGE — HAVASU CITY
2. SUNSET CRATER NATIONAL MONUMENT
3. MONUMENT VALLEY
4. LITTLE COLORADO RIVER AND PAINTED DESERT
5. GRAND CANYON

ARKANSAS

CAPITAL -
LITTLE ROCK

25th. STATE
JUNE 16, 1836

AREA -53,104 sq. miles
-137,539 sq. km.

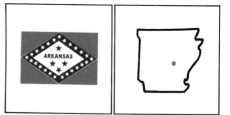

Arkansas, a south central state, was part of the Louisiana Territory which France sold to the United States in the famed Louisiana Purchase of 1803.
The Ozark and Ouachita Mountains form the northern and western part of the state. The southeastern half is part of the Gulf Coastal Plain, and this rich, fertile land is ideal for growing cotton and rice.
Many people believe that the mineral spring waters of Arkansas will cure certain ailments. One of the most famous cities Hot Springs, is world-renowned for its health centers.
The only diamond field in North America is found in Murfreesboro, and is a popular place for tourists to visit.
During the Civil War Arkansas elected to join the Confederacy. However, the decision was not unanimous, and there was a split between the two factions. Until the end of the War, Arkansas had two governments — one Union and one Confederate.
Today the state's greatest industry is food processing. It ranks third among all the states in cotton production... and is an important supplier of lumber and wood products.
Mother Nature has endowed Arkansas with beautiful lakes, sparkling streams, majestic mountains and scenic waterfalls-making it a very attractive state to live in and visit.

HOT SPRINGS

The Indians first called Hot Springs "The Valley of Vapors" - a very appropriate name, since the area has 47 thermal springs. The first explorer known to visit Hot Springs was Hernando De Soto in 1541. The city is world-renowned for its many health spas which provide relief for people who suffer from arthritis and various muscular disorders. A great resort and convention center, as well as health center, Hot Springs provides visitors with unlimited recreational opportunities.

BUFFALO RIVER STATE PARK

This beautiful park encompasses 2,160 acres of Ozark Mountains, and features springs, caves, nature trails, and the famous Buffalo River - one of the nation's few remaining free-flowing streams. Offering a breathtaking experience to canoeists, the river extends for 132 miles in a serpentine course.

1. HOT SPRINGS
2. BUFFALO RIVER STATE PARK

CALIFORNIA

CAPITAL -
SACRAMENTO

31st. STATE
SEPTEMBER 9, 1850

AREA -158,693 sq. mil.
-411,015 sq. km.

California, nicknamed the "Golden State", is a land of many terrains. Its Mount Whitney, which is 14,495 feet high, is the highest place in the country (outside of Alaska). And Death Valley —only 85 miles away —is the lowest point in the country, lying 282 feet below sea level.

Three quarters of California is made up of mountains, hills and plateaus. The remaining quarter consists of level land below 500 feet in elevation. The Pacific coastline is 1,200 miles long, and is bordered by a coastal plain. The only major indentations in the coast are Monterey Bay and San Francisco Bay —one of the world's finest harbors.

The vegetation of California is as gorgeous and varied as its land structures. In the far south one can find a select variety of tropical growth... and a wide variety of cacti in the deserts. The central region is valuable timber country, noted for its redwoods and sequoias. These trees grow 200 to 300 feet high, and have trunks that measure 15 to 20 feet in diameter.

13

2

3

4

Just north of San Francisco lies the Napa Valley, where the vineyards supply a major share of grapes for wine; making California one of the world's largest wine producers.

Recreational facilities abound in this state, and visitors can choose from beautiful beach resorts along the scenic coastline; the mountains, offering both summer and winter activities; the splendid national parks and forests; or the numerous desert resorts.

The missions located throughout the state are a result of the efforts of two Franciscan priests, Father Junipero Serra and Father Fermin Laseur. By 1823 they had built 21 missions from San Diego to Sonoma. These missions provided the first real growth in California.

After the Mexican Revolution in 1822, Spanish rule was ended and Californians swore allegiance to Mexico —but remained self-governing. There was much unrest between northern and southern California, due to the region's 23-day stand as an independent republic.

The United States flag was raised in Monterey, and statehood was granted in 1850 . . . at the height of the gold rush. Sacramento became the capital in 1854.

SAN FRANCISCO

One of the most charming cities in the world, San Francisco is noted for its Cable Cars, streets bedecked with flower carts, and exciting, exotic Chinatown. Telegraph Hill, providing a bird's-eye view of the entire North Bay, is the site of the 210-foot Coit Memorial Tower. And the Golden Gate Bridge, one of the longest suspension bridges ever built —with the highest towers in the world, spans the Golden Gate Strait, connecting San Francisco with Marin County and the Redwood Highway.

QUEEN MARY —LONG BEACH

Launched by King George of England in 1934, the Queen was used during World War II to carry soldiers home and abroad. After the war she was renowned as one of the most luxurious cruise ships in the world.

HEARST CASTLE—SAN SIMEON

Construction of the Hearst Castle was begun in 1919 by William Randolph Hearst, who first occupied it in 1925. The grounds and dwellings are located at the top of La Cuesta Encantada (the Enchanted Hill), a 600-foot mountain with a view of San Simeon and the Pacific Ocean. Now a State Historical Monument, the Hearst Castle is open to the public for tours.

LOS ANGELES

The largest city in California, highly-urbanized Los Angeles is renowned for its diverse activities —ranging from oil-processing and aircraft-manufacturing to orange growing, television and movie-making.

SEQUOIA NATIONAL PARK

Located in the Sierra Nevadas between San Joaquin and Owens Valley, it is the site of Mount Whitney, highest peak in the continental United States. Heavily forested with large trees, the park contains the Giant Forest, largest of the sequoia groves —with the 270-foot high General Sherman Tree, said to be around 3,500 years old. First discovered in 1858 by rancher Hale Tharp, the Sequoia Forests were visited by United States naturalist John Muir in 1875. The park was established in 1890.

MOUNT SHASTA

Rising to a height of 14,162 feet, Mount Shasta is the site of several glaciers, everlasting snowfields, large timberlands and a hot spring (located near the summit).

Located in the Shasta-Cascade Wonderland in northern California; Mount Shasta is woven with ski runs ... as well as with many trails for summer hikers.

MOUNT WHITNEY

Located in the Sierra Nevadas, this is the highest peak in the continental United States, rising to a height of 14,495 feet. This mountain range forms the eastern boundary between Sequoia National Park and Kings Canyon National Park.

KINGS CANYON NATIONAL PARK

A land of giant canyons, numerous lakes, waterfalls and mountain meadows, Kings Canyon National Park is the steep-walled, 9-mile-long valley at the south fork of the Kings River. The park contains many large forests of giant sequoia trees. The largest of these, the General Grant Tree, stands 267 feet high, has a diameter of over 40 feet, and dates back to 1600 B.C. Many trails are provided to give hikers easy access to the heart of the magnificent mountains and lake regions.

1. GOLDEN GATE
2. SAN FRANCISCO
3. QUEEN MARY — LONG BEACH
4. HEARST CASTLE — SAN SIMEON
5. LOS ANGELES — CITY HALL AND «THREE THEATRE» MUSIC CENTER
6. SEQUOIA NATIONAL PARK
7. MOUNT SHASTA
8. MOUNT WHITNEY
9. KINGS CANYON NATIONAL PARK

7

8

9

5

6

COLORADO

CAPITAL - **DENVER**
38th. STATE
AUGUST 1, 1876

AREA -104,247 sq. mil.
-270,000 sq. km.

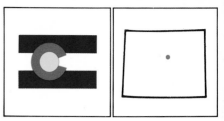

1

2

Colorado is the highest state above sea level. Denver is known as the "Mile High City". Quite often referred to as the "Rocky Mountain State", Colorado is also known as the "Centennial State", because it was admitted to the union in 1876 —during our nation's 100th birthday.
The state is divided into 3 distinct physical regions —the Colorado Plateau in the west, the Rocky Mountains in the center and the Great Plains in the east. The Continental Divide, which runs through the west central portion of the state, separates the rivers flowing west from those flowing east. Colorado's industries are mainly associated with its agriculture and its mineral resources. The surrounding mountains provide ideal locations for many winter resort areas.
Col. Zebulon M. Pike led the first American exploration party into Colorado in 1806; and fur traders started establishing posts in the state in the 1830's.
The discovery of gold in 1858, and later discoveries of silver, started a rash of settlements and mining towns to spring up —as thousands headed west in search of their fortunes. Colorado became a territory of the United States in 1861 and a state in 1876.

GREAT SAND DUNES NATIONAL MONUMENT
Located in the San Luis Valley at the western slope of the Sangre de Cristo Mountains, the Great Sand Dunes National Monument encompasses an area of 36,740 acres. Blown by prevailing westerly winds, the ever-changing sand dunes rise to a height of about one thousand feet, and are among the largest and highest dunes in the United States.

AIR FORCE ACADEMY
The Air Force Academy is located at the foot of the Rampart Range of the Rocky Mountains, 12 miles north of Colorado Springs. Graduating its first class in June 1959, it is the newest of the service schools.

MESA VERDE NATIONAL PARK
Mesa Verde National Park is 15-20 miles in size, rising 1800 to 2000 feet above the valley on the north side. It slopes gradually to the steep cliffs that border the Mancos River Canyon on the south. Mesa Verde, Spanish for "green table", has an almost level top, which is forested with juniper and pinon trees. Located in southwestern Colorado, it is one of the nation's major archaeological preserves.

PIKES PEAK
Pikes Peak was discovered by Col. Zebulon M. Pike in 1806, and was scaled by Maj. Stephen H. Long in 1820. Pikes Peak is 14,110 feet of reddish granite, easily visible from far out on the Great Plains. Located on the southern Front Range of the Rocky Mountains, it is accessible by horse, auto or cog railway.

ROCKY MOUNTAIN NATIONAL PARK
Rocky Mountain National Park contains 3 major mountain ranges —Front Range, extending north-south; the Mummy Range in the northeast; and the Never Summer Range in the northwest. Included in its 259.876 acres are 65 named peaks of more than 10,000 feet in elevation . . . plus several small glaciers. Located in the Front Range is Longs Peak, rising to a height of 14,255 feet, making it the highest point in the park.

1. GREAT SAND DUNES NATIONAL MONUMENT
2. AIR FORCE ACADEMY
3. MESA VERDE NATIONAL PARK
4. PIKES PEAK
5. ROCKY MOUNTAIN NATIONAL PARK

3

4

5

CONNECTICUT

CAPITAL -
HARTFORD

5th. STATE
JANUARY 9, 1788

AREA -5,009 sq. miles
-12,973 sq. km.

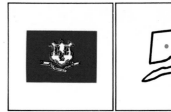

Connecticut encompasses an area of 5,009 square miles, and is located in the northeastern corner of the United States. Although it is small in size, it has a diversified terrain of mountains, wooded hills, lakes, and 618 miles of coastline. For the history student, it offers many historical sites and museums.

The people of Connecticut played an important role in the early history of our country. They were staunchly patriotic and strong in their religious views. When General Washington needed troops during the Revolutionary War, Connecticut answered the call by sending the majority of her men to his army, thus supplying one half of the total number to the cause.

Today Connecticut is foremost in manufacturing, with the largest percentage of industrial workers of all the states. It is also known as the "insurance capital" of the world. Tobacco is the chief agricultural product.

GILLETTE CASTLE—HADLYME

Located in Gillette Castle State Park, this huge fieldstone mansion is reminiscent of Europe's medieval castles. Built as a private home, it was erected in 1919 by Victor William Gillette, an actor well-known for his portrayal of Sherlock Holmes for 30 years.

COAST GUARD ACADEMY—NEW LONDON

The Academy is located on a 100-acre tract on the west bank of the Thames River. Each year hundreds of cadets are graduated and commissioned as ensigns in the Coast Guard . . . the nation's oldest sea-going force, dating back to 1790.

1. GILLETTE CASTLE — HADLYME
2. COAST GUARD ACADEMY — NEW LONDON
3. MYSTIC SEAPORT

DELAWARE

CAPITAL - **DOVER**
1st. STATE
DECEMBER 7, 1787
AREA -2,057 sq. miles
-5,328 sq. km.

Delaware, the first of the original 13 colonies, was the first state to ratify the United States Constitution. It lies at the northeastern corner of the southern states region, along the Atlantic coastline.

Indians of the Algonkian tribes were the first inhabitants. The first settlers came from Holland in 1631, and were followed by the Swedish in 1638, who built Fort Christina (where Wilmington is today). In 1664 Delaware came under English rule. By the mid 1700's, the white settlers had forced most of the Indians to move.

Today Delaware is a leading producer of chemicals. Wilmington, known as the "chemical capital of the world", is the home of the Dupont Company, one of the world's largest industrial organizations.

DELAWARE MEMORIAL BRIDGE

This bridge was erected across the Delaware River as a memorial to the more than 14,000 American soldiers from Delaware and New Jersey who gave their lives during World War II. Each name is inscribed in

3

1

2

bronze. This double suspension span permits rapid transportation to the eastern New Jersey shore, and to many historic and resort areas of Delaware. One of the longest suspension bridges in the world, it is more than two miles long, and is suspended 190 feet above the water.

FORT DELAWARE

Located near Delaware City on Pea Patch Island, this fort was built in 1859. During the Civil War it served as a Federal prison. Today it is part of the Fort Delaware State Park.

OLD TOWN WILMINGTON

Settled by the Swedes in 1638, Wilmington is now the leading chemical-producing area of the world, and corporate charter home of many of America's largest companies.

1. DELAWARE MEMORIAL BRIDGE
2. FORT DELAWARE
3. OLD TOWN WILMINGTON

FLORIDA

CAPITAL -
TALLAHASSEE

27th. STATE
MARCH 3, 1845

AREA -58,560 sq. miles
-151,670 sq. km.

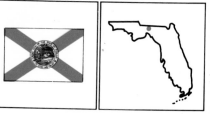

1

Florida means "Full of Flowers" in Spanish, and was so named by Ponce de Leon, the Spanish explorer who discovered the Florida territory in 1513. Looking for the legendary "Fountain of Youth", he didn't realize what a paradise he really found.

Sunshine, palm trees, white sand beaches and orange groves are synonymous with Florida.

Florida produces three quarters of all the oranges grown in our nation, and grapefruit is also high on the list in production. And Florida is one of the nation's leading suppliers to the commercial fish industry.

The "Sunshine State" has played a very important role in the Space Age — beginning with the first U.S. earth satellite, launched from Cape Canaveral in 1958, to our joint space expedition with the Russians.

The state has much to offer in the way of a vacation —whether it's sun bathing on Miami Beach . . . or touring Disney World. It's a Land of Sunshine —making it an ideal place to visit or live in.

MIAMI BEACH

Known as the "Gold Coast", Miami Beach is one of Florida's busiest resort areas . . . with miles of sandy white beaches and famous hotels. Basking in the sun, swimming in the ocean, horse racing and fishing are just some of the many activities available year round.

KENNEDY SPACE CENTER—CAPE CANAVERAL

Cape Canaveral, located at Cocoa Beach, is the nation's major space and rocket center. The first American earth satellite was launched from here in 1958. Since then, many successful space flights have been launched, including the Apollo "Walk on the Moon" and the U.S.-Russian joint space flight in 1975.

ST. AUGUSTINE

St. Augustine is the oldest city in the United States. First visited by Ponce de Leon in 1513, it was settled by Pedro Menéndez de Avilés, a Spanish explorer, in 1565. Located on the Atlantic coast in northeast Florida, the city has many fine beaches and historic sites to visit, like castillo San Marcos National Monument.

THE EVERGLADES

The mighty Everglades River, often called the "River of Grass", flows from Lake Okeechobee south to the sea. A multitude of animals and over 230 species of birds can be found here. The Everglades became a national park in 1947. Encompassing an area of 2,188 square miles, it is the largest subtropical wilderness in the United States.

2

1. MIAMI BEACH
2. KENNEDY SPACE CENTER — CAPE CANAVERAL

3. WALT DISNEY WORLD
4. ST. AUGUSTINE
5. THE EVERGLADES

3

4

5

GEORGIA

1

2

Georgia's size ranks 21st among all the states, and is the largest of all eastern states. Her capital, as well as her largest city, is Atlanta.

Called the "Empire State of the South" because of her thriving industry, Georgia is a leading producer of cotton, pecans and tobacco. Another customary nickname is the "Peach State" because of her high production of peaches. Peanuts are another leading agriculture product.

Not only is the state known for her industrial and agricultural contributions, but for her breathtaking countryside, as well. Georgia's topography includes everything from the picturesque mountains in the north to the misty sea coast. Many quaint villages dot the Atlantic shore; and the beaches — along with other attractions — delight vacationers throughout the year.

JEKYLL ISLAND
Nestled on the Georgia coast, it has long been the site of fervent incidents in our history. In 1886 a group of America's wealthiest families —aware of the agreeable climate, pure water and natural beauty —bought Jekyll for their exclusive winter retreat. However, in 1947 the state of Georgia purchased the island. Today everyone is welcome to share in the healthy, entertaining recreation.

Golfing, beaching, tennis and fishing are only a few of the pleasures one can enjoy on this enchanted isle.
STONE MOUNTAIN
Located east of Atlanta in Stone Mountain Park, this massive dome of muscovite granite is five miles in diameter, and rises 825 feet above the surrounding plain. The immense carving on its north face the largest in the world, honors the Confederate soldiers who were dedicated to the cause of the South during the Civil War. General Robert E. Lee, leader of the Confederate armies, is depicted on his faithful horse, Traveler. This carving makes Stone Mountain known as the "Mount Rushmore of the South".
BRASSTOWN BALD
The highest point in Georgia at 4,784 feet, Brasstown Bald is located in the northern Georgia Blue Ridge Mountains.

1. JEKYLL ISLAND
2. STONE MOUNTAIN
3. BRASSTOWN BALD
4. I-85 LAKE HARTWELL
5. ATLANTA

3

4

5

HAWAII

CAPITAL -
HONOLULU

50th. STATE
AUGUST 21, 1959

AREA -6,450 sq. miles
-16,706 sq. km.

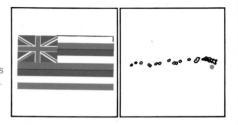

1

When Hawaii became a state, the focus of the world centered on this tiny chain of islands in the middle of the Pacific Ocean. Honolulu is the capital, and also the largest city. It is approximately 2,400 miles southwest of the U.S. mainland.

The first settlers came to these islands about 800 A.D., bringing their gods, history and customs. Called Polynesians, they were from the nearby South Pacific. Then others came from the Orient, from America, and from all over the world. As a result, the harmonious blending of the races has produced a civilization.

Hawaii is the only state of the United States that is made up entirely of islands. Each of the 4 principal islands is unique in its own way. Hawaii, the largest, has the volcanic mountains of Mauna Loa and Mauna Kea, which rise to a height of almost 14,000 feet. Lush rain forests and many cattle ranches dot the landscape. Maui is popular for its magnificent beaches and beautiful national park. Kauai, called the "Garden Island" for its wonderful array of growing things, is also noted for its long white beaches and rugged mountains. Molokai, one of the smaller islands, has a wealth of wildlife —making it ideal for outdoor sportsmen. The Halawa Valley has a lush vegetation and beautiful waterfalls that form natural swimming pools. The last one, Lanai, called the "Pineapple Island" because of its many pineapple plantations, also has fine beaches. Each of the eight principal islands are unique in its own way. Oahu is the main island as it includes Honolulu, the Capital City, and 80% of the state's population.

2

3

DIAMOND HEAD

This extinct volcano, rising to a height of 761 feet, was once used as burial grounds for ancient Hawaiians. Today its familiar form provides a dramatic backdrop to the world-famous resorts of Honolulu and Waikiki Beach. In the foreground is the graveyard of the Pacific.

THE U.S.S. ARIZONA MEMORIAL—PEARL HARBOR

This World War II Memorial is built directly over the hulk of the sunken Battleship Arizona. Entombed below deck are nearly 2,000 sailors who lost their lives in the surprise attack by the Japanese on December 7, 1941.

HALEAKALA NATIONAL PARK

Located on Maui, this is the island's highest point, and the world's largest volcanic crater —25 miles around and nearly 3,000 feet deep. The observation area in the foreground is reached by highway from Kahului.

KILAUEA VOLCANO

This volcano erupts frequently, sending fiery lava down to the ocean. From the Hawaiian Island Observatory, scientists study the volcanic activity of Kilauea in the Hawaii Volcanoes National Park.

1. DIAMOND HEAD — OAHU
2. MAUNA KEA RESORT
3. THE U.S.S. ARIZONA MEMORIAL — PEARL HARBOR
4. HALEAKALA NATIONAL PARK
5. PINEAPLE PLATATION — LANAI
6. KILAUEA VOLCANO

4

5

6

IDAHO

CAPITAL - **BOISE**

43rd. STATE
JULY 3, 1890

AREA -83,557 sq. miles
-216,413 sq. km.

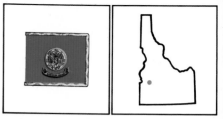

1

1. KETCHUM
2. CASTLE PEAK WITH STANLEY BASIN AREA
3. CRATERS OF MOON NATIONAL MONUMENT
4. MESA FALLS — NEAR YELLOWSTONE NATIONAL PARK

2

3

4

The name Idaho is from the Shoshone Indian words "ee dah how" which means "the sun comes down the mountain". It is an apt name, since over half of the state is covered by primitive and massive snow-covered mountain ranges.

Known for producing the famed "Idaho Potatoes", Idaho also produces millions of dollars worth of minerals. "The Gem State" has the nation's largest silver and lead mine. Gold, diamonds, rubies, coal and lead are just some of the minerals and rare gems found in Idaho. Indians lived in this region thousands of years ago —according to markings found in caves, and other evidence uncovered by archaeologists. In 1805 Lewis and Clark were the first white men to explore the region. After 1860, when Ed Pierce found gold in Orofino Creek, towns mushroomed overnight all over Idaho. Farmers and cattlemen followed the miners to Idaho. When the miners exhausted the immediate supply of gold and moved on, the farmers and cattlemen stayed to develop the area.

KETCHUM
Located near Sun Valley, Ketchum is one of Idaho's major ski areas. Ernest Hemingway lived here while writing his famous novels.

CASTLE PEAK WITH STANLEY BASIN AREA

45 miles east of Challis is Stanley Basin, one of Idaho's favorite recreational areas. Breathtaking beauty surrounds the Basin, with lovely alpine meadows and an abundance of lakes —some of which cut long inlets deep into Sawtooth Wilderness. Castle Peak, with an elevation of 11,820 feet, towers majestically over this recreational area —where one can find excellent camping and boating facilities.

CRATERS OF THE MOON NATIONAL MONUMENT
This 83-square-mile region of pock-marked desolation has long reminded man of its similarity to the crater-faced moon. It is bordered by a sagebrush plateau, sparsely sprinkled with stunted pines . . . and it is a great expanse of lava, cinder cones, and more than 60 volcanic craters. On the eastern horizon one can spot the looming Big Southern Butte —while the Pioneer Mountains and Lost River Range rise on the north. Craters of the Moon, pushed up out of the earth by volcanic eruption, stands at an elevation of 7,576 feet.

MESA FALLS—NEAR YELLOWSTONE NATIONAL PARK
Scenic Mesa Falls, located on the North Fork of the Snake River, has an upper drop of 114 feet and a lower drop of 65 feet.

27

ILLINOIS

CAPITAL -
SPRINGFIELD

21st. STATE
DECEMBER 3, 1818

AREA -56,400 sq. miles
-146,076 sq. km.

1

Illinois was first discovered by two French explorers, Father Jacques Marquette and Louis Jolliet, in 1672. For almost 100 years the French dominated the area, and established good rapport with the Indians until the British defeated them and claimed the Illinois territory for England.

The giants of industry, men like Cyrus H. McCormick and George M. Pullman, are synonymous with the early development of the state. Today Illinois is a great manufacturing state.

In the University of Chicago laboratory, the atomic age was launched in 1942. Chicago is the state's largest city, and more than half the state's population is centered there.

The state has numerous lakes and rivers, beautiful forests, rolling countryside, and 63 miles of scenic shoreline around Lake Michigan. These natural attractions are inviting to the tourists.

LINCOLN'S NEW SALEM STATE PARK—SPRINGFIELD
At Lincoln's New Salem State Park the visitor can find a reproduction of the town in which Abraham Lincoln lived from 1831-1837. Some of the reproduced buildings are the tavern and store in which he was a part owner, and the old "cooper" shop where Lincoln studied at night.
The park lies northwest of Springfield.

CHICAGO
Chicago, along Lake Michigan's southwest shore boasts O'Hare airport as the world's busiest and claims the highest buildings in the world, the Sears Towers.

DIXON INDIAN MOUND
One of many Indian Mounds found in Illinois. Remains uncovered here disclosed a fairly advanced way of life and some form of government.

1. LINCOLN'S NEW SALEM STATE PARK—SPRINGFIELD
2. CHICAGO
3. LINCOLN BURIAL SITE
4. DIXON INDIAN MOUND

3

4

INDIANA

1

2

3

4

The people in Indiana chose as their state motto "The Crossroads of America", because of its central location. In comparison to other states, Indiana is small in area and large in population.

The first white man to explore the region (in 1679) was a Frenchman named Rene Robert Cavalier, Sieur de la Salle. In 1731 the French built a permanent settlement in Vincennes. The constant struggle between

30

the French and English —over the lucrative fur trade with the Indians —ended in France giving Indiana to the English to colonize and settle.

Today Indiana is a great manufacturing state, especially noted for its production of steel. Agriculture ranks second, making Indiana important in the production of corn.

Rolling hills and fertile plains make up the terrain of Indiana. It is a state of great natural beauty, which makes it attractive to the vacationer. Artists, particularly, like to paint the Indiana landscape as it changes colors from one season to another.

INDIANA SAND DUNES
The great Sand Dunes border Lake Michigan's shore just east of Gary, and provide vacationers with miles of swimming and sunning fun.

TIPPECANOE—BATTLEGROUND
After a series of events, the power of the Indians was broken on this battleground. It was here that the Shawnee Prophet, Brother of Shawnee Chief Tecumseh, was defeated by a militia led by William Henry Harrison — then Indiana's governor. Later, in his quest for the

presidency, he and his running mate, John Tyler, inspired voters with their slogan "Tippecanoe and Tyler Too".

2 OF 33 COVERED BRIDGES
Parke County, in west central Indiana, holds the record for the most covered bridges. It has over 33, and boasts the longest free span in the country —which is 207 feet long. This reminiscence of the 1800's provides hours of entertainment as the tourist literally goes out of one bridge into another.

INDIANAPOLIS MOTOR SPEEDWAY
Since 1911 the Speedway has attracted millions of speed enthusiasts who thrill to the 500 miles of nearly 200-mile-per-hour speeds. Names of racers like A. J. Foyt, Al Unser, Mario Andretti, Lee Roy Yarbrough, Wilbur Shaw and Eddie Rickenbacker are synonymous with the heroes of this famous classic.

1. INDIANA SAND DUNES
2. TIPPECANOE—BATTLEGROUND
3. 2 OF 33 COVERED BRIDGES
4. INDIANAPOLIS MOTOR SPEEDWAY

5

IOWA

CAPITAL -
DES MOINES

29th. STATE
DECEMBER 28, 1846

AREA -56,290 sq. miles
-145,791 sq. km.

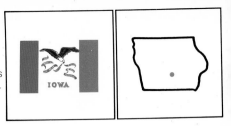

Iowa was called "Beautiful Land" by its first inhabitants, the Indians. At one time 17 Indian tribes made Iowa their home. Included in the Louisiana Purchase of 1803, Iowa became part of the Missouri Territory in 1812, following expeditions by Lewis and Clark.

The richness of the soil makes Iowa one of our best farming states. Sometimes called the "Corn State", it grows about 1/5 of the nation's supply of corn. Iowa's manufacturing industries, closely tied to its agriculture, include meat processing, farm machinery, dairy products and processing of food products.

Some of Iowa's most famous "favorite sons" were: Herbert Hoover, 31st President; Henry Wallace, Vice-President under Franklin D. Roosevelt; and Grant Wood, one of the greatest painters of all times.

Iowa is a state for all seasons, with the mighty Mississippi River on the eastern boundary and the equally grand Missouri River to the west. Beautiful forests, lakes, streams and rolling prairies make up the terrain of the "Hawkeye State". Beginning with the Indians and blending with the pioneers with their varied ethnic backgrounds, Iowa has a fascinating history that adds to the uniqueness of its people and its land.

LITTLE BROWN CHURCH IN THE VALE—NASHUA

William Pitts, a young music teacher, wrote the song "The Little Brown Church in the Vale" after passing through a tranquil setting in which he envisioned a church. When he returned to the same location several years later, he was surprised to see that his "vision" had become a reality. The Little Brown Church is one of Iowa's most visited tourist places, and many weddings are performed in its charming, rustic atmosphere. And the song written by William Pitts has grown in popularity through the years.

NEW MELLERAY ABBEY

This Cistercian-Trappist monastery is located on rolling farmland, 12 miles southwest of Dubuque. It is a religious order founded by monks in 1849, who came from Ireland seeking peace and solitude. The Gothic-style stone buildings house some fifty monks of the Cistercian order, who support themselves by farming and cattle raising.

EFFIGY MOUNDS NATIONAL MONUMENT

These unusual Indian mounds are located near Marquette, and contain 1,374 acres. They extend for 3 miles along the bluffs of the Mississippi River. This aerial view shows the mound in the shape of a bear. Similar ones are shaped like other animals. These mounds contain the remains of prehistoric Indians who lived in this region more than a thousand years ago.

LAKE OKOBOJI

This unique lake is spring fed, reaching a depth of 134 feet, and gets its truly blue color from blue algae. Largest and most beautiful of the blue water lakes, it ranks with Switzerland's Lake Geneva and Canada's Lake Louise.

1

2

3

4

5

6

1. LITTLE BROWN CHURCH IN THE VALE—
   NASHUA
2. NEW MELLERAY ABBEY
3. EFFIGY MOUNDS NATIONAL MONUMENT
4. IOWA FARMS
5. BLUFFS ALONG THE MISSISSIPPI RIVER
6. LAKE OKOBOJI

33

KANSAS

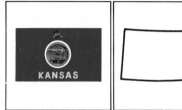

1

Kansas was untouched by the white man for many years, until the Louisiana Purchase in 1803 opened up the territory for exploration and settlement. At first, the move to Kansas was mainly political, since the slavery question was a hot issue, and North and South jostled for control. There was a constant conflict between the pro and anti slavery forces until Kansas entered the Union as a free state in 1861.

When Samuel Ward wrote about "amber waves of grain" in his immortal "America The Beautiful", he was probably thinking of Kansas. With her crops dotting the prairies for endless miles, Kansas leads all the state in the production of wheat. An important industrial state as well, she ranks among the six leading states in petroleum and natural gas production; and also produces over half of the nation's aircraft.

Nicknamed the "Sunflower State", Kansas is an Indian word meaning "people of the south wind". Dodge City, one of her most famous towns, is referred to as the "Cowboy Capital of the World". During the 1860's through 1880's, Dodge City was the cattle market of the world. Here, too, the legends grew of men like Wyatt Earp, Wild Bill Hickock and Masterson.

DODGE CITY

Dodge City was reputed to be one of the wildest and roughest towns on the frontier. Today one can see a carefully reproduced version of Dodge City in its heyday —complete with Front Street and Boot Hill.

FORT LARNED NATIONAL HISTORIC SITE

Built in 1859 by the U.S. Army, this fort was established to protect settlers and mail shipments - passing along the Santa Fe Trail - from Indian raiders. Later, the fort guarded construction crews working on the Santa Fe Railroad. After the railroad was completed, in 1878, the fort was abandoned. In 1964 Fort Larned became a National Historic Site and part of the National Park System. You can still see ruts from the wagon trains in the fields along the side of the fort.

WICHITA

The "Aircraft Capital of the World", Wichita is the home of Cessna, the leading aircraft company.

1. SUNSET ON THE MISSOURI RIVER
2. DODGE CITY
3. FORT LARNED NATIONAL HISTORIC SITE
4. WICHITA

2

3

4

KENTUCKY

CAPITAL -
FRANKFORT

15th. STATE
JUNE 1, 1792

AREA -40,395 sq. miles
-104,623 sq. km.

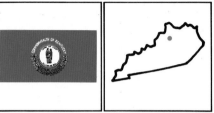

1

2

3

Kentucky stayed in the Union during the Civil War, but many of her sons joined the Confederacy. The Kentucky of today is a major manufacturing and agricultural state. It is second to North Carolina in the production of tobacco, and third in coal production. The nation's gold reserves are stored in underground vaults at Fort Knox. In May the strains of "My Old Kentucky Home" are heard in the air, and the bugle signals the start of another Kentucky Derby at Churchill Downs in Louisville. Horses like Man O' War and Secretariat raced here and made racing history. Travelling past the lush, Blue Grass pastures covering the hills around Lexington, you can see the graceful thoroughbreds frolicking in the fields. Moving along, you can see fields of tobacco growing in the warm sun . . . and you can take the road to Bardstown, where some of the world's finest whiskey is distilled.

Kentucky is a beautiful state, with many lakes and caves to explore. Mammoth Cave National Park, the mountains and woodlands are all ideal for nature lovers, or those who just want to find that old pioneer spirit.

RED RIVER GORGE
Within easy reach of the Mountain Parkway, southeast of Lexington and near Natural Bridge, is the Red River Gorge, an area of rugged cliffs, lively streams, woods and rare plant life.

CUMBERLAND FALLS
Located near Corbin, this is Kentucky's highest waterfall. It plunges 68 feet into the Cumberland River, and is the largest waterfall —next to Niagara Falls— in the eastern United States.

BELLE OF LOUISVILLE
The Belle of Louisville is and old-fashioned stern-wheeler that still cruises the Ohio River. During the Derby festival in May, a favorite event is a race between the "Belle" and the "Delta Queen".

LEXINGTON HORSE FARMS
Horse farms in and around Lexington are numerous, and many are open to the public. Some of the most famous farms are: Calumet Farm, Derby Dan Farm, Spendthrift Farm, and Domino Farm shown here.

1. RED RIVER GORGE
2. CUMBERLAND FALLS
3. BELLE OF LOUISVILLE
4. LEXINGTON HORSE FARMS

LOUISIANA

CAPITAL -
BATON ROUGE

18th. STATE
APRIL 30, 1812

AREA -48,523 sq. miles
-125,675 sq. km.

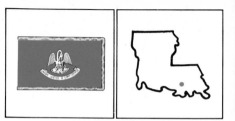

1

2

Shaped like a boot with its toe pointed eastward, Louisiana lies where the Mississippi River empties into the Gulf of Mexico. Waterways link the state with the heart of America . . . as well as with countries across the sea . . . making Louisiana one of the nation's busiest commercial areas.

Her largest city, New Orleans, ranks as one of the world's busiest ports. The Mississippi River can carry ocean ships 235 miles to the state capital of Baton Rouge. Oil and natural gas wells are an important part of Louisiana, and represent the greatest source of her wealth. In 1960 Louisiana became an important Space Age industrial center.

Louisiana's lifestyle is based on its variety of peoples, cultures and customs. Every year throngs of visitors come to New Orleans for the gay carnival season and the famous Mardi Gras. Here tourists can enjoy the versatility of her French and Spanish quarters, and delight in the New Orleans style of jazz.

CHALMETTE NATIONAL HISTORICAL PARK

Part of these grounds were the scene of the Battle of New Orleans. During this battle, Jackson successfully defended the city against the British, gaining enough popularity to bring him to the presidency. This area was established as Chalmette Monument and Grounds in 1907, and received its present designation in 1939. The site of the Battle of New Orleans is marked by a 100-foot memorial shaft. Inside the park is the Chalmette National Cemetery, a military burial ground.

OAK ALLEY PLANTATION

A magnificent road lined with huge oak trees leads the way to Oak Alley Plantation. Built in 1836, it is one of Louisiana's oldest and finest mansions.

JACKSON SQUARE

Originally known as the Place d' Armes, Jackson Square has been the center of New Orleans since 1720. Named in honor of Andrew Jackson after the Battle of New Orleans, the square today is a public park with frequent performances by jazz bands and other musical groups. After acquiring the Lousiana Territory, the American flag was raised for the first time in Jackson Square.

FORT McCOMB

Located east of New Orleans, this fort defended New Orleans from 1819 to 1828.

1. CHALMETTE NATIONAL HISTORICAL PARK
2. OAK ALLEY PLANTATION
3. JACKSON SQUARE — NEW ORLEANS
4. RICE FIELDS
5. FORT McCOMB

3

4

5

MAINE

CAPITAL -
AUGUSTA

23rd. STATE
MARCH 15, 1820

AREA -33,215 sq. miles
-86,027 sq. km.

1

2

3

4

Maine is the largest of the New England states. The Appalachians extend across the center of Maine, making her a state of rolling and hilly country. The state is said to contain 2,465 lakes and ponds - as well as a large number of rivers and streams. Many beautiful beaches are located along her southern tip's rocky coastline. The forests of Maine cover 85% of the state, making her land the largest per capita acreage in the nation. Her unspoiled scenery makes Maine one of the country's most splendid vacation spots. The state is known for her boating and water sports in the summer . . . and is a winter paradise for skiing and other snow activities. John Smith's expedition in 1614 explored, mapped and named the area "New England". In 1677 Massachusetts purchased the Province of Maine from the heirs of Ferdinando Gorges, one of Maine's first proprietors. The Treaty of 1814, following the War of 1812, settled most of the borders of the Maine-Massachusetts region. In 1819

another border was formed, and Maine separated from Massachusetts. Statehood was granted in 1820.
ACADIA NATIONAL PARK
Acadia National Park contains 40 square miles of Mount Desert Island, the largest rock-based island on the Atlantic coast. Rising abruptly from the sea, this beautiful mountain park is the highest elevation along the Atlantic seaboard. The park contains 15,000 acres of fresh water lakes; and the granite mountains are covered with pine forests and a wide variety of wildflowers. In Acadia National Park one will be able to see Somes Sound, the only fiord on the Atlantic coast of the continental United States.

1. ACADIA NATIONAL PARK
2. TYPICAL FISHING VILLAGE
3. QUODDY LIGHT
4. BEAVER DAM

MARYLAND

CAPITAL -
ANNAPOLIS

7th. STATE
APRIL 28, 1788

AREA -10,577 sq. miles
-27,394 sq. km.

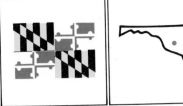

Maryland, known as the "Old Line State", has a colorful history going back to Cecil Calvert, the second Lord Baltimore. In 1634 he claimed the land as a haven for Catholics, who were being persecuted in England. For its relatively small size, Maryland has a variety of terrain with Chesapeake Bay as the most distinguishable feature. The state is known for its exceptionally fine harbors. Baltimore, the largest city, has one of the greatest ports in the world.

Most of Maryland's wealth comes from manufacturing and commerce. Known for its fine seafood, especially around the Chesapeake Bay area, it is a leading producer of soft-shelled crabs and oysters.

Some of America's finest thoroughbreds come from the lush Bel Air pastures, and these are a source of pride to Maryland.

Two of the most popular vacation areas in the state are along the Atlantic shore and in the beautiful Allegheny Mountains.

1

3

ANNAPOLIS NAVAL ACADEMY
The Academy has more than 1,100 acres on the banks of the Severn River. It was established in 1845 by Goerge Bancroft, Secretary of the Navy under President James K. Polk. Many of our nation's finest men are graduated each year from the Academy.

FORT FREDERICK
Located 10 miles west of Hagerstown, in Fort Frederick State Park, this massive stone fortress was built during the French and Indian Wars. It has reigned over the Potomac River since 1757.

FORT McHENRY -NATIONAL MONUMENT AND HISTORIC SHRINE
Built between 1798 and 1803, this fort has served our country in every war through World War II. During the War of 1812, the British were determined to capture the fort at any cost, since it was vital to the defense of Baltimore. While the fort was under heavy bombardment, Francis Scott Key wrote the national anthem, "The Star Spangled Banner".

1. ANNAPOLIS NAVAL ACADEMY
2. FORT FREDERICK
3. FORT McHENRY — NATIONAL MONUMENT AND HISTORIC SHRINE

2

MASSACHUSETTS

CAPITAL - **BOSTON**
6th. STATE
FEBRUARY 6, 1788
AREA -8,257 sq. miles
-21,386 sq. km.

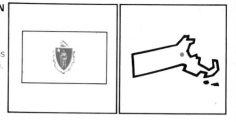

1. BOSTON COMMONS
2. BOSTON LIGHT
3. PROVINCETOWN—CAPE COD
4. LEXINGTON AND CONCORD BRIDGE
5. PLYMOUTH ROCK

Massachusetts received its name from the Massachuset Indian Tribe which lived in the region when the Pilgrims arrived. Its historic beginning is well-remembered for the Mayflower landing on December 21, 1620. Although ships had landed before this date, the Mayflower was the first to remain. Massachusetts' drive for economic development and personal freedom is well-preserved in her wealth of historical documentation. She has been appropriately nicknamed the "Bay State" and the "Colony State".

She is among the top manufacturing states of today. Boston, the capital city, is a major U. S. seaport and air terminal.

The terrain is a series of hills and valleys; and more than half the nation's cranberries come from her farms.

BOSTON COMMONS

The oldest public park in the country, it was bought by the people in 1634 for common use as a cow pasture and training field. Incidents included in her colorful past are: the mustering of British troops before the Battle of Bunker Hill; and, in the 17th Century, the hanging of pirates, witches and Quakers from the "Old Elm", located near the Frog Pond in the center of the park. Stocks and pens used by the Puritans to punish those who violated the Sabbath are still standing to this day.

PROVINCETOWN—CAPE COD

Located at the tip of Cape Cod, this was the site of the first Pilgrim landing. Today the Pilgrim Memorial Monument commemorates the temporary landing of the Pilgrims in 1620. Once an important whaling town, Provincetown is an important fishing town today, and the home of one of the best known Colonial art collections in the country.

LEXINGTON AND CONCORD BRIDGE

Lexington Green was the site of the first skirmish of the Revolutionary War, held on April 19, 1775 . . . between the Minutemen and Concord-bound British soldiers. Visitors coming into Lexington will more than likely follow the path of Paul Revere on his Midnight Ride. Just beyond Lexington lies the Concord Bridge and Daniel French's famous statue of "The Minutemen". Here the embattled farmers stood and fired the "shot heard around the world".

PLYMOUTH ROCK

Sitting in the Bay of Plymouth Rock is the Mayflower II —an authentic reproduction of the original ship. In December of 1620, 102 settlers landed in Plymouth. After their first winter, only 50 Pilgrims were known to have survived the extreme cold and hunger. During the month of August, residents of Plymouth dress in Pilgrim garb and climb Burial Hill to hold a simple ceremony in memory of the 50 survivors.

3

4

5

MICHIGAN

CAPITAL - **LANSING**

26th. STATE
JANUARY 26, 1837

AREA -58,216 sq. miles
-150,779 sq. km.

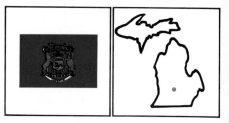

1

2

3

1. TAHQUAMENON FALLS
2. MACKINAC BRIDGE
3. ISLE ROYALE NATIONAL PARK
4. PICTURE ROCKS, LAKE SUPERIOR—
5. SAULT SOO LOCKS AT SAULT STE. MARIE
6. NEW PRESQUE ISLE LIGHTHOUSE AND PARK

The French were the first to send explorers to the
Michigan territory in the 1600's. They held onto the
region for about 150 years, but did nothing to develop it.
They were mainly interested in Christianizing the Indians
and arguing with the British over the fur trade in North
America. The dispute finally ended in 1754, when
the French lost control to the British in the French
and Indian Wars.

Touching four of the five Great Lakes, including
Lake Michigan, the largest in the U.S., Michigan has
more water in it than any other state. Its two distinct
land features, the Upper Peninsula and the Lower
Peninsula, are connected by the Mackinac Bridge built
in 1957.

Michigan is the leading automobile manufacturing state.
Detroit, the largest city, is called the "Automobile
Capital of the World". It is also a leading tourist state,
offering the finest in resort and recreational facilities.
With 11,000 smaller lakes and forests, that comprise
more than half the state, Michigan is rich in scenic
beauty as well as in industrial might.

TAHQUAMENON FALLS
The Tahquamenon Falls has played a colorful role
in the early history of this area. Longfellow referred
to the Tahquamenon in his poem about "Hiawatha". The
falls are within easy driving distance from the towns
of Sault Ste. Marie and St. Ignace.
The main stream of the Tahquamenon is 94 miles long;
its tributaries total 545 miles in length. With its
abundance of wildlife, feeding along the winding
shores, it offers visitors unlimited opportunities of
sight-seeing or sport participation. This scenic
wonderland can be visited by canoe or riverboat.

MACKINAC BRIDGE
In 1955 work began on the Mackinac Straits Bridge,
linking Michigan's two peninsulas together. This bridge
is the longest suspension bridge in the world, spanning
five miles across the Straits of Mackinac.

PICTURE ROCKS, LAKE SUPERIOR.
These colorful rocks form all shapes and sizes as they
curve for 20 miles eastward, starting at Munising —on
the North Shore's Upper Peninsula overlooking Lake
Superior. Composed mostly of stratified sandstone and
seeping metallic oxides, the rocks represent some of
nature's finest in scenic history.

SAULT SOO LOCKS AT SAULT STE. MARIE
Constructed in 1855, these locks transformed the once
raging St. Mary's River into one of the world's most
efficient waterways. A 21-foot elevation between Lake
Superior and Lake Huron necessitated the building of
these locks. Today more have been added to allow the
passage of 4 ships an hour. The Soo Locks are operated
by the U.S. Army Corps. Boat cruises are popular
through these locks —because of the many points of
interest on both the Canadian and American shores.

NEW PRESQUE ISLE LIGHTHOUSE AND PARK
The new "Presque Isle Lighthouse" was built in 1870,
about a mile north of the "old lighthouse". It is
automatically controlled and under the supervision of
the Coast Guard. The white conical tower stands 109
feet high at the northern tip of the peninsula, and is
surrounded by a 98-acre park. A narrow road leading
to the lighthouse makes it easily accessible to visitors.

4

5

6

MINNESOTA

CAPITAL - **ST. PAUL**

32nd. STATE
MAY 11, 1858

AREA -84,068 sq. miles
-217,736 sq. km.

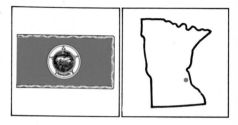

The largest of the mid-western states, Minnesota comes from a Sioux Indian word meaning "sky-tinted".

The first white men came to Minnesota in the late 1600's. Here they found the Sioux Indians living peacefully as farmers and hunters. One of the early explorers, a Frenchman named Sieur Duluth, entered Minnesota in 1679 and claimed the entire territory for King Louis XIV of France.

Today Minnesota is one of our chief food-producing states. Its main manufacturing activity is processing the products of its many farms. The state also ranks high in the production of iron ore and lumber.

Minneapolis is the largest city, and St. Paul is the capital. Often called the "Twin Cities", they are the leading cultural, financial and commercial centers for the state.

Minnesota is a land of scenic beauty —with sparkling lakes and deep, pine-tufted forests. It is truly a winter wonderland, with white powdery snow and ice making it perfect for winter sports. It is an ideal place to live in or to visit —any season of the year!

SPLIT ROCK LIGHTHOUSE STATE PARK
Located about 50 miles north of Duluth on Highway 61, the historic Split Rock Lighthouse is a unique attraction.

HIBBING IRON MINE
This is one of the world's largest open pit iron ore mines. The hole is about 3 1/2 miles long, 1 1/4 miles wide and 500 feet deep. Most of the iron ore is mined by the open pit method, since the ore lies close to the surface.

GOOSEBERRY FALLS STATE PARK
One of the most popular waterfalls in Minnesota, Gooseberry Falls is located on Route 61, along the Lake Superior shoreline. This state park gets its name from the many-leveled falls along both sides of scenic Route 61, just north of Duluth.

PIPESTONE NATIONAL PARK
This national park encompasses 238 acres. The Indians discovered this quarry, using the stone to make pipes. This skilled craft, passed on from one generation to another, is still being practiced today. In legislation signed by Franklin D. Roosevelt on August 25, 1937, quarrying rights, rather than mineral rights, were reserved for the Indians of all tribes.

1. SPLIT ROCK LIGHTHOUSE STATE PARK
2. HIBBING IRON MINE
3. GRAND PORTAGE NATIONAL HISTORIC SITE
4. GOOSEBERRY FALLS STATE PARK
5. PIPESTONE NATIONAL PARK
6. IRON ORE RANGE WITH RAINBOW

4

5

6

MISSISSIPPI

CAPITAL -
JACKSON

20th. STATE
DECEMBER 10, 1817

AREA -47,716 sq. miles
-123,584 sq. km.

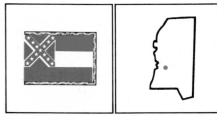

1

2

Mississippi is a land of enchantment. Spanish Moss, magnolia trees, stately pillared homes, and cotton fields dot the landscape; and all are preserved forever in the history of this deep South state.

Today Mississippi is more of an industrial state, with factories and bustling cities . . . a far cry from the plantations of the 1800's. Farming is still important to the state's economy, however, and a variety of crops and livestock are raised there. The northwestern part of Mississippi produces the most cotton, and is one of the greatest cotton producing areas in the nation.

FORT MASSACHUSETTS

Located 12 miles off the Mississippi Gulf Coast on Ship Island, this fort guards the entrance to Biloxi Bay, which was vital to the Union blockade of the South. It was also used as a Union prison for some 6,000 Confederate soldiers. This landmark was named for the Union Steamboat "Massachusetts", which successfully attacked the fort during the Civil War.

BAY ST. LOUIS BRIDGE
Looking East along U. S. Highway 90, this $9.000.000.00
Bridge opened Aug. 1, 1953. It is over two miles long
and connects Bay St. Louis and Pass Christian, Miss.
INGALL'S SHIPBUILDING
Among the world's most modern ship-builders, Ingall's
builds Atomic powered Submarines for the U.S. Navy,
General Purpose Ships and Commercial Vessels.
MISSISSIPPI GULF COAST
Winter or summer, the Mississippi Gulf Coast
is a popular place for vacationers, who enjoy the tangy
salt breezes and sandy beaches. In the foreground
is the historic Biloxi Lighthouse and the town of Biloxi.

1. FORT MASSACHUSETTS
2. BAY ST. LOUIS BRIDGE
3. INGALL'S SHIPBUILDING
4. MISSISSIPPI GULF COAST

3

4

MISSOURI

CAPITAL -
JEFFERSON CITY

24th. STATE
AUGUST 10, 1821

AREA -69,686 sq. miles
-180,487 sq. km.

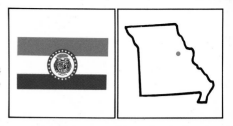

'1

2

In 1803 the United States bought the Louisiana Territory from France. After the Louisiana Purchase, settlers started to arrive in numbers to the new Missouri territory.

Missouri is sometimes called the "Frontier of the West", since thousands of pioneers began their journey westward from there in the early 1800's. Famous routes like the Oregon Trail and the Santa Fe began in Independence.

It is an ideal state to live in geographically, because it is here that the country's two greatest rivers join. The mighty Mississippi meets the great Missouri just above St. Louis. The rivers played a meaningful role in establishing Missouri as an important shipping state in early times. They are equally important today as a major force in the state's economy.

The traveler will see a variety of terrain, from rolling plains of golden grain and lush green grass to the rugged hills of the Ozarks further south —with winding streams and wooded plateaus. In the Ozarks one will find colorful mountain people with a culture distinctly their own.

One cannot leave Missouri without being reminded of the great legacies left to her and to our nation by such notables as: Harry S. Truman, 33rd President; Mark

Twain, beloved novelist; George Washington Carver, esteemed scientist; and Thomas H. Benton, famous painter.

LAKE OF THE OZARKS AND BAGNELL DAM

One of the world's largest man-made lakes, this ranks among America's best-known vacation areas. This aerial view of the lake and dam shows the 1,375 miles of shoreline . . . with its countless nicks and coves, which is why it is sometimes called mid-Missouri's "dragon".

ST. LOUIS ARCH

Erected on the grounds of the Jefferson National Expansion Memorial, this arch commemorates St. Louis' role as "Gateway to the West". Constructed of gleaming stainless steel, it soars 630 feet above the mall. Designed by Eero Saarinen, it is 75 feet higher than the Washington Monument. Specially-designed equipment and 886 tons of stainless steel were required to build it.

HANNIBAL

Located on the west bank of the Mississippi River, 120 miles north of St. Louis, Hannibal is the boyhood home of Mark Twain. A growing metropolis supported by industry and agriculture, it is a far cry from the small Missouri town that Mark Twain knew.

1. LAKE OF THE
   OZARKS AND
   BAGNELL DAM
2. COVERED
   BRIDGE AND MILL
   NEAR CAPE
   GIRARDEAU
3. ST. LOUIS ARCH
4. HANNIBAL

4

MONTANA

CAPITAL - **HELENA**
41st. STATE
NOVEMBER 8, 1889

AREA -147,138 sq. mil.
-381.087 sq. km.

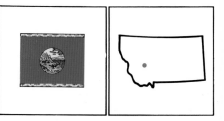

1

Nicknamed the "Treasure State", this fourth largest state in the union is a state of abundant wealth —usually associated with the gold and silver still found in the Montana mountains . . . along with copper, petroleum, coal and rare earth metals. More than 2 billion tons of soft coal lie under Montana.
Helena, the state capital, has a reputation for wealth that stems from the early mining days. Her main street, Last Chance Gulch, is named after the gold mining camp that stood on that site. Even today, when a basement is dug for a new building in Helena, the digging produces enough gold to pay for the building.
Back when Montana belonged to the Indians, gold and silver prospectors intruded into a beautiful wilderness which contained bountiful game and shelter for tribes such as the Sioux and Cheyenne. Indian troubles started in the 1860's —when wagon trains were attacked and mining camps raided. In 1876 the government sent the 7th Cavalry, under Col. George Custer, against the Sioux and Cheyenne. On June 25, 1876, on the banks of the Little Big Horn River, the Indians massacred Custer's entire troop. This was the battle that became known as "Custer's Last Stand".
In 1877 another major Indian battle was fought at the Big Hole in southwest Montana. There the Nez Perce Indians, under Chief Joseph, fought bravely, then retreated . . . surrendering to General Nelson Miles.

GLACIER NATIONAL PARK

Montana has 2 major land regions, the Great Plains and the Rocky Mountains. The Rocky Mountains cover two fifths of Montana. With long narrow valleys of one to five miles wide and 30-40 miles long, the Rocky Mountains harbor an agricultural region . . . as well as Glacier National Park. The Park consists of 1.583 square miles of Rocky Mountains. It has over 900 trails, where 25,000 hikers and campers annually backpack, hike and climb their way through scenic beauty. Once a huge glacier formed the rugged terrain of Glacier National Park, but today 60 glaciers dot the million acres of parkland.
The Park has beautiful lakes, waterfalls, forests and meadows. Moose, deer, bear, coyote, bighorn sheep, mountain goat, cougar and fish are the kinds of wildlife a backpacker spots along the trail on the 50 miles of Going-to-the-Sun road. Hiking, camping, biking, boating, swimming, fishing and mountain climbing are activities open for 3 months —June 15 to September 15— in the Glacier National Park.

FAMOUS OPEN PIT

Much of Montana's growth during the 1880's and 1890's was due to the gold mines in Butte. Early mines in Butte Hill produced gold, then silver, and then rich veins of copper. Butte Hill soon became known as the "Richest Hill on Earth". Now Butte continues its history of mining with the famous Berkeley Open Pit. Under the city are over 9,000 linear miles of mines that have yielded almost 4 billion dollars in ores.

1. BIG HORN MOUNTAINS
2. GLACIER NATIONAL PARK
3. FAMOUS OPEN PIT — BUTTE

3

NEBRASKA

CAPITAL - **LINCOLN**
37th. STATE
MARCH 1, 1867
AREA -77,227 sq. miles
-200,018 sq. km.

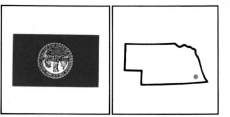

1

2

3

The Nebraska territory was originally part of the Louisiana Purchase. In 1804 President Thomas Jefferson sent an expedition, headed by Lewis and Clark, to explore the eastern part of Nebraska. Then, in 1806, Zebulon M. Pike explored the south central region. Nebraska was called "the great American Desert" at one time, and was considered by many to be unsuitable for farming. When the first pioneers came in the early 1860's, they found the area quite difficult to farm. Through perseverance and determination, however, they overcame the obstacles of drought, insects and plain hard times —turning the land into productive farms. Today Nebraska is one of the leading agricultural states, with corn the largest single crop. Land unsuitable for growing crops is used for cattle raising. Her chief manufacturing activities involve the processing of foods and related products. Omaha is considered one of the largest meat packing centers in the world.
Nicknamed the "Cornhusker State", from the many cornhusking contests held each fall in the rural communities, Nebraska is the only state with a unicameral state legislature, meaning one house.
Every year thousands of vacationers flock to Nebraska, traveling on highways that were once the historic Oregon and Mormon Trails. Many wagon ruts from the past can still be seen today.

SCOTTS BLUFF NATIONAL MONUMENT
Scotts Bluff is a massive point of land, rising 800 feet above the valley and 4,649 feet above sea level. Named in honor of a fur trapper named Hiram Scott, who died in the vicinity around 1828, the bluff is an ancient landmark —used by the different Indian tribes, as well as by pioneers as they journeyed west.

CHIMNEY ROCK NATIONAL HISTORIC SITE—BAYARD
This massive natural monument rises about 500 feet above the North Platt River, and was a landmark for pioneers moving westward on the Oregon Trail.

MITCHELL PASS
Mitchell Pass is an area that was used by the Pony Express riders in 1860-1861. Later on, the first transcontinental telegraph lines were built through here. Fort Mitchell, established 2 1/2 miles to the northwest, protected stagecoaches and wagon trains from Indian raids along the Oregon Trail.

1. SCOTTS BLUFF NATIONAL MONUMENT
2. CHIMNEY ROCK NATIONAL HISTORIC SITE — BAYARD
3. MITCHELL PASS

NEVADA

CAPITAL -
CARSON CITY

36th. STATE
OCTOBER 31, 1864

AREA -110,540 sq. mil.
-286,299 sq. km.

Nevada lies in the Great Basin, an area of long, narrow and rugged mountain ranges with intervening valleys and basins. The highest point, Boundary Peak, rises 13,145 feet; and the lowest point, the southern region of the Colorado River, is only 470 feet above sea level. Nevada is the driest state in the country. Rivers are small in volume, and some waterways only flow during and after scarce seasonal rainfalls. The Colorado River flows along the southern border; and the Humboldt River, the longest river originating in Nevada, flows from east to west for nearly 300 miles, ending in the Humboldt Sink. Lake Mead, the country's largest artificial lake, is formed by Hoover Dam on the Colorado River. It lies on the Nevada-Arizona border.

For years Nevada was discounted as a dry and desolate land, but the discovery of gold in 1850 at Carson City brought this land to life. Then in 1859 the Comstock Lode, one of the richest deposits of gold and silver ever discovered, caused Nevada to become a boom state. Once part of the Utah territory, Nevada became its own territory in 1861. Due to its fastspreading fame, it was granted statehood in 1864.

LAS VEGAS

Las Vegas, the entertainment center of the world, is also the gambling capital. Starting as a Mormon settlement, it boomed during the silver rush. The arrival of the railroad in 1905 kept Las Vegas from becoming another ghost town. The legalization of gambling in 1931 resulted in a springing up of casinos throughout the downtown area. Today Las Vegas draws over 15 million visitors a year to its fabulous resort hotels and casinos along the famous Las Vegas Strip . . . offering a wide variety of famous celebrities and numerous specialty shows.

HOOVER DAM

Impounding Lake Mead, and rising 726 feet high, Hoover Dam is one of the highest dams ever constructed, and is recognized as one of the greatest engineering projects in the world. Water stored in the dam irrigates farmland in Arizona and parts of southern California. Crossing a crest of the dam itself, visitors can view Hoover Dam from both sides of the Black Canyon. Elevators are available to carry visitors into the dam for a tour of the power plant.

LAKE TAHOE

One third of Lake Tahoe lies within Nevada; the remaining two thirds lie in California. Measuring 22 miles long and 12 miles wide, the lake lies in a valley between the main Sierra Nevada and the Carson Range, an eastern offshoot.

1. LAS VEGAS   2. HOOVER DAM   3. LAKE TAHOE

NEW HAMPSHIRE

CAPITAL -
CONCORD

9th. STATE
JUNE 21, 1788

AREA -9,304 sq. miles
-24,097 sq. km.

1

New Hampshire, the "Granite State", is the most mountainous of all the New England states. Tucked away in the northeast corner of the United States, her many mountain ranges, clear lakes and sparkling beaches make her a year round vacation sport — with a wide variety of recreational activities.

The second most industrialized state in the union per capita, her economy relies mainly on manufacturing. Agriculturally, her production of cattle and poultry is used at home and abroad.

In January 1774 New Hampshire declared her independence from Great Britain. She was the first state to adopt her own constitution, and the 9th state to accept the Federal Constitution. Her motto, "Live Free or Die", depicts the moral attitude of her people — who have fostered educational, economic and social progress through the years.

FRANCONIA NOTCH

Franconia Notch is one of the most famous mountain gaps in the East. Containing 6,440 acres of deep valley, this notch lies between the lofty peaks of the Franconia and Kinsman mountain ranges.

GREAT STONE FACE

Discovered in 1805, the "Great Stone Face" is a natural phenomenon which shows the profile of a man's face jutting from a sheer cliff — 1200 feet above Profile Lake. Formed by the evolution of nature thousands of years ago, the face measures about 40 feet from chin to forehead.

BRETTON WOODS HOTEL

This famous White Mountain resort was the scene of the Bretton Woods Conference — the United Nations Monetary Conference held in July 1944.

MOUNT WASHINGTON

Rising 6,288 feet in the Presidential Range of the White Mountains, this is the highest peak in New England

HAMPTON BEACH

Hampton Beach covers 2 miles of the Atlantic seashore. Along this strip of beach are 2 state developments. The Sea Shell, a modern complex in the heart of the Hampton Beach resort area, contains a band shell and amphitheatre. Hampton Beach State Park, which lies north of the resort area, contains many up-to-date facilities to accommodate its many visitors.

2

1. FRANCONIA NOTCH
2. GREAT STONE FACE
3. BRETTON WOODS HOTEL
4. MOUNT WASHINGTON
5. HAMPTON BEACH

3

4

5

NEW JERSEY

CAPITAL - **TRENTON**

3rd. STATE
DECEMBER 18, 1787

AREA
-7,836 sq. miles
-20,295 sq. km.

1

New Jersey is of great economic importance to the United States. Her location between the Hudson and Delaware Rivers provides miles of wharves and docks, servicing ocean liners and freighters from the United States and abroad. New Jersey leads the country in the production of chemicals, and supplies a variety of products to many countries of the world. Her agricultural products are the main source of supply for poultry, fruit and vegetables to the northeastern states. Contrasting her industrial cities are more than fifty resort cities and towns along her beautiful coastline.

WASHINGTON CROSSING PARK

Established to commemorate George Washington's famous crossing of the Delaware River, this 795-acre park is located 8 miles north of Trenton, in Mercer County. Along with its many picnic facilities, the park also houses the McKoney Berry Farm House Museum, the Flag Museum in the McKoney Barn, the Nature Center and a theater.

FORT MOTT

This 104-acre State Park, located near Salem on the Delaware River, offers picnicking, boating and fishing facilities.

1. WASHINGTON CROSSING PARK
2. FORT MOTT
3. BARNEGAT LIGHTHOUSE
4. ATLANTIC CITY

2
BARNEGAT LIGHTHOUSE

From 1834 to 1927 the Barnegat Lighthouse warned mariners of the nearby treacherous waters of the Atlantic Ocean. Today it is a favorite subject for painters and photographers. Standing 172 feet high, and containing a 217-step spiral staircase, the lighthouse draws many visitors to her top, where one can see a breathtaking view of the ocean and the bay.

ATLANTIC CITY

One of the largest seaside resorts in the world, Atlantic City lies 140 miles south of New York City and 60 miles southeast of Philadelphia. Its famous boardwalk, which is 60 feet wide and stretches 7 miles along the oceanfront, is lined with theaters, casinos, restaurants, hotels and Convention Hall — where the Miss America pageant is held every year. Five large piers, which extend off the boardwalk, provide amusement places, public parks and exhibits for the many tourists.

3

4

NEW MEXICO

CAPITAL -
SANTA FE

47th. STATE
JANUARY 6, 1912

AREA -121,666 sq. mil.
-315,115 sq. km.

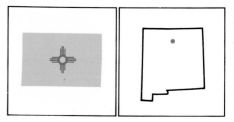

1

2

Nicknamed the "Land of Enchantment", New Mexico is the 5th largest state in the union. Her terrain can best be described as a rolling plain dotted with mountain ranges. The Sangre de Cristo Mountains are the site of Wheeler Peak, the highest peak in the state, rising to a height of 13,161 feet. The arid terrain of New Mexico is watered by the Rio Grande, Pecos and Canadian Rivers and tributaries of the Colorado River — providing fertile, grassy plains for the grazing of cattle. The most famous of New Mexico's natural wonders is the national park of the Carlsbad Caverns. These caves were formed by the constant flow of underground streams wearing away the thick layers of limestone.

In New Mexico, sheep and cattle outnumber people two to one, and ranching is her main industry. Mining is also important, and New Mexico leads the nation in the production and reserves of uranium.

In 1848, 2 years after Gen. Stephen Kearny captured Santa Fe, New Mexico became a territory of the United States. During the Civil War, Texas volunteers attempted to seize New Mexico in an attempt to extend the Confederate territory to the Pacific coast. Their defeat to the Union soldiers caused their retreat.

RIO GRANDE GORGE
A stronghold for one of America's great rivers, the Rio Grande Gorge is a 70-mile-long north/south notch in north central New Mexico. Soaring 600 feet above the water, the Rio Grande Gorge High Bridge spans the canyons, and is the only rim-level automobile crossing of the wild river.

GILA CLIFF DWELLINGS NATIONAL MONUMENT
Surrounded by Gila National Forest, this national monument lies at the edge of Gila Wilderness Area. The earliest monument found within this area is a pit house of a type used from 100 to 400 A.D. It contains the living quarters of the "Cliff Dwellers" who built their homes in natural caves —as well as the houses of the Pueblo people.

WHITE SANDS NATIONAL MONUMENT
Located in the Tularosa, this national monument

encloses part of White Sand, the largest of the rare gypsum deserts. Shimmering, snow-white sand dunes, rising 10 to 40 feet high, are found within these 146.535 acres. Dry winds evaporate the gypsum which collects in Lake Lucerne and blows the crystallized particles into the surrounding area — causing frequent changes in the appearance of the dunes. Vegetation is scarce, with only a few varieties able to survive the constant changing of the sands. The only inhabitants are mice and lizards, whose white skins help them blend into the landscape.

ACOMA PUEBLO AND MISSION

Often referred to as the "Sky City", Acoma is located atop a great sandstone rock, almost 400 feet high. The Indians established themselves at or near the present location as early as 900 A.D., and the pueblo has been continually inhabited since 1075. In 1629 Father Ramirez won the hearts of the Indians, and constructed a mission church which was called San Estevan. During a rebellion, the church was almost completely destroyed, but it was rebuilt to be used as a place of worship again. The men of Acoma are primarily cattle ranchers and farmers; the women are noted for their fine pottery.

SHIPROCK

Closely connected with Indian legend and mythology, Shiprock rises more than 1,700 feet above the desert floor. This oddly-shaped rock is so named because of its apparent ability to glisten and float under the glow of the evening's setting sun.

1. RIO GRANDE GORGE
2. GILA CLIFF DWELLINGS NATIONAL MONUMENT
3. WHITE SANDS NATIONAL MONUMENT
4. TAOS PUEBLO
5. SHIPROCK
6. ACOMA PUEBLO AND MISSION

3

4

6

5

NEW YORK

CAPITAL - **ALBANY**
11th. STATE
JULY 26, 1788
AREA -49,576 sq. miles
-128,402 sq. km.

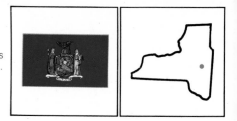

1

2

In 1609 Henry Hudson sailed up the Hudson River and laid claim to this virgin land in the name of Holland. Called New Netherland, this colony bought Manhattan Island from the Indians for about $24. England took over in 1664, and remained in control until the Revolutionary War.

One of the 13 original colonies, New York played a major role in the war. After the Revolution, New York City became the nation's first capital, and George Washington took his oath of office there as first President of the United States.

New York is a state for all seasons. Mountains, sparkling lakes, rivers and forests are all part of her natural beauty . . . as are her Niagara Falls, which attracts millions of visitors annually.

It is a foremost state in manufacturing, commerce and foreign trade. New York City is the home of Wall Street, the largest financial district in the world. It is also the scene of the world's biggest and busiest seaport, and the most beloved landmark of all: The Statue of Liberty, gracing the harbor with her torch of freedom.

STATUE OF LIBERTY
A symbol of Liberty and a shining ray of hope to the millions of people who have passed by her in New York Harbor, the Statue of Liberty was a gift from the people of France, and was dedicated in 1886.

FORT TICONDEROGA
Located on Lake Champlain, this famous fort was taken over by Ethan Allen during the American Revolution.

BASEBALL HALL OF FAME — COOPERSTOWN
This national landmark is located in James Fenimore Cooper's hometown —where baseball's first game was played in 1839.

ERIE CANAL
Completed in 1825, this artificial waterway connects the Hudson River with Lake Erie.

WEST POINT
This U.S. Military Academy is the oldest military college in the United States. The Academy has 16,000 acres on the west bank of the Hudson River. Each year West Point has graduated many fine officers, who have distinguished themselves down through the years in the service of our country.

NIAGARA FALLS
One of the world's natural wonders, the magnificent splendor of the Falls attracts millions of visitors each year. About 500,000 tons of thundering water plunge over the Falls each minute. Horseshoe Falls, on the Canadian side, is even larger than the American Falls. Several observation towers have been built here to give spectators more of a bird's-eye view.

1. STATUE OF LIBERTY
2. WALL STREET
3. MIDTOWN MANHATAN

4

5

6

7

4. FORT
   TICONDEROGA
5. BASEBALL
   HALL OF FAME—
   COOPERSTOWN
6. ERIE CANAL
7. WEST POINT
8. NIAGARA
   FALLS

1. WORLD GOLF
   HALL OF FAME
   — PINEHURST
2. USS NORTH
   CAROLINA
3. BILTMORE
   HOUSE AND
   GARDENS —
   ASHEVILLE
4. MOUNT MITCHE
   STATE PARK — 6

NORTH CAROLINA

CAPITAL - **RALEIGH**

12th. STATE
NOVEMBER 21, 1789

AREA -52,586 sq. miles
-136,198 sq. km.

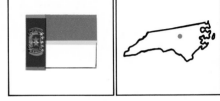

A magnificent cross section of land containing all that is the "best" in North America, North Carolina is almost 53,000 square miles in area - about the size of England. Located just south of Virginia and washed by the waters of the Atlantic Ocean on the east, it extends 500 miles to the west with a width of 187 miles at its widest point. North Carolina, known as the "Tar Heel State", is divided into three distinctive sections. Along the Atlantic, for a depth of more than a hundred miles, is the Coastal Region. Here the sand and surf provide fun in the sun from May until mid-autumn.

WORLD GOLF HALL OF FAME — PINEHURST
Sitting amid majestic pines, the World Golf Hall of Fame is dedicated to honoring the immortals of the game, and enhancing its centuries-old heritage. The magnificence of this golf shrine makes it one of the greatest in the world.

USS NORTH CAROLINA
Permanently moored across the Cape Fear River from downtown Wilmington, the USS North Carolina Battleship Memorial is open daily, and attracts thousands of visitors annually to tour the ship's 8 decks and levels open to the public.

BILTMORE HOUSE AND GARDENS — ASHEVILLE
One of the finest mansions in America, the home of the late George W. Vanderbilt, was opened to the public in 1930 as a memorial to him. Biltmore House took 5 years to build and was completed in 1895. The estate once included 145,000 acres, and now covers 12,000 acres.

MOUNT MITCHELL STATE PARK
Dominating the Black Mountain Range, this is the highest peak in the eastern half of the country - rising over 6,684 feet. It offers an outstanding view . . . along with nature trails, camping facilities and an excellent restaurant.

1

2

3

4

NORTH DAKOTA

CAPITAL -
BISMARCK

39th. STATE
NOVEMBER 2, 1889

AREA -70,665 sq. miles
-183,022 sq. km.

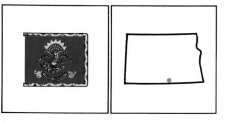

North Dakota is primarily a plain state, with the western section lying in the central plains. The Red River Valley, which extends the length of the eastern border, has the lowest elevation in the state. Black Butte, rising 3.468 feet, is the highest point in North Dakota.

Primarily an agricultural state, the most favored section for farming is the Red River Valley. Farms are generally large, averaging 755 acres. In 1959 North Dakota had more than 54,000 farms, covering almost 42 million acres. Sharing the Williston Oil Basin with Montana, North Dakota ranks 9th in oil reserves —with producing wells located in 13 western counties. An estimated 350 billion tons of lignite, one of the largest hard fuel reserves in the nation, makes low-grade coal a major resource for North Dakota.

Recreational facilities abound in North Dakota —with Lake Sakakawea, Lake Oahe and the Missouri River among the major vacation spots. The mountains provide hiking, camping and hunting, and the national parks draw many visitors all year round.

The first permanent settlement was Pembina, which was occupied by British subjects displaced by the Industrial Revolution. Fort Union, established in 1829 at the merging of the Yellowstone and Missouri Rivers, served as headquarters for the Upper Missouri Outfit —whose primary purpose was a rendezvous for traders, trappers and Indians. Succeeded by Fort Buford, a U.S. Army Post, this was the site of Sitting Bull's surrender in 1881. When the great Sioux chief surrendered, 3 decades of Indian unrest came to an end. The Dakota territory consisted of both North and South Dakota. Because of unresolved disputes over rights to the capital city, the territory was divided into 2 portions, and both were admitted to the Union as separate states.

MEDORA—HEART OF THE BADLANDS

Medora is located in the Badlands, one of the country's finest natural wildlife reserves. Founded in 1883 by a wealthy French nobleman, the Marquis de Mores, the town has restored historic buildings for modern day use. Theodore Roosevelt came to this area in 1883 and established a ranch which is now part of the Theodore Roosevelt National Park.

THEODORE ROOSEVELT NATIONAL PARK

This park is full of scenic beauty, with an abundance of weird and brightly-colored formations. Erosion has mingled gray, blue, red and brown colors that provide a breathtaking view during morning and late evening hours. Located in the Badlands of North Dakota, this 70,436-acre park pays tribute to contributions made by Theodore Roosevelt toward the conservation of our nation's natural resources.

OHIO

CAPITAL -
COLUMBUS
17th STATE
MARCH 1, 1803
AREA -41,222 sq. miles
-106,765 sq. km.

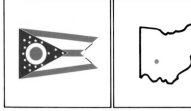

Ohio was one of the first territories that the tightly-knit 13 original colonies ventured forth to explore. The Ohio River made exploration of this inland state a less difficult task.

The primary eastern tributary of the Mississippi River, the Ohio River made the region strategic in every phase of our nation's evolution. With other streams and canals, it furnished the nautical highway for exploration and trade; and the power for industrial development. Lake Erie, together with the St. Lawrence Seaway, provided the deep-water harbors that have made Ohio significant in world commerce.

U.S. AIR FORCE MUSEUM —DAYTON
Exhibits tell the history of aviation, beginning with the first flight at Kitty Hawk. Displays also deal with the atomic bomb and Gemini Series space capsules. The Museum tour features a view of approx. 100 different types of aircraft, including: the only remaining B-70, the aircrafts of Presidents Truman and Eisenhower, World War II planes, fighters used in Viet Nam, and other foreign aircraft.

PERRY'S VICTORY AND INTERNATIONAL PEACE MEMORIAL
Located on South Bass Island at Put-In Bay in Lake Erie, this is an awesome sight. It stands 352 feet high and measures 45 feet in diameter at its base. The monument commemorates the Battle of Lake Erie, fought during the War of 1812; and the ensuing years of peace between English-speaking peoples.

PRO-FOOTBALL HALL OF FAME —CANTON
Inside this football-shaped building, visitors will view busts of outstanding players, hear a recording of Jim Thorpe's voice, and see a 30-minute film on football — featured to inform young and old alike about America's most popular sport.

1

2

1. U.S. AIR FORCE MUSEUM— DAYTON
2 PERRY'S **VICTORY** AND **INTERNATIONAL PEACE** MEMORIAL
3. PRO FOOTBALL HALL OF FAME

1. MEDORA — HEART OF THE BADLANDS
2. THEODORE ROOSEVELT NATIONAL PARK

3

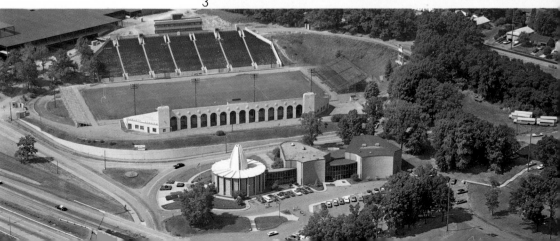

OKLAHOMA

CAPITAL -
OKLAHOMA CITY

46th. STATE
NOVEMBER 16, 1907

AREA -69,919 sq. miles
-181,090 sq. km.

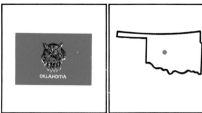

1

2

3

Oklahoma comes from two Choctaw Indian words: Okla - people, and homa - red. It is known as the "Sooner State", because settlers arrived sooner than the official opening of the land as a white settlement. Oklahoma City, the state capital, is the largest city in population, as well as the largest in area, covering more than 649 square miles.

The state has vast reserves of minerals and large areas of fertile soils. The earliest cultivated lands belonged to the early cliff dwellers who lived in Oklahoma. Millions of Hereford Cattle graze on Oklahoma's plains. Its oil and gas wells provide products valued at 800 million dollars a year.

"Coronado, 1541" was found inscribed on the wall of a cavern in Oklahoma, which proves that Coronado passed through here in search of the legendary "Seven Cities of Cibola". The Five Civilized Tribes — Cherokee, Choctaw, Creek, Chickasaw and Seminole — received their Oklahoma lands from the federal government for "as long as the grass shall grow and the rivers run" —in return for their eastern lands. "The Trail of Tears" is the trail that the Indians followed in their forced migration into their new western territories. Many thousands of Indian men, women and children lost their lives during the long trek in freezing weather.

The greatest Oklahoma land rush occured at the opening of the Cherokee Outlet on September 16, 1893. More than 50,000 persons staked claims the first day.

DEEP SEAPORT — TULSA
This deep seaport transports much of the petroleum that Tulsa controls. It is the control center for one quarter of the nation's petroleum industry. Formerly a Creek Indian village, Tulsa was incorporated in 1896. It grew very slowly until oil was discovered at nearby Red Fork.

WILL ROGERS' SHRINE —CLAREMORE
"There ought to be a law against anybody going to Europe until they have seen the things we have in this country." Will Rogers was talking about the United States, but he could easily have been thinking of his beautiful homeland, Oklahoma. Built by the state of Oklahoma on land donated by Mrs. Rogers, this shrine - which is open to the public free of charge - commemorates the man who gave many smiles and witticisms to our country.

BLACK MESA
Black Mesa State Park, established in 1959, has a history that began millions of years ago — when prehistoric beasts, such as the 65-foot-long Brontosaurus, roamed the area. Black Mesa State Park, with its Indian history, is located in Cimarron County in northwest Oklahoma. Lava from an extinct volcano forms the setting of Black Mesa — which is just short of 5,000 feet above sea level, and the highest point in Oklahoma.

PAWNEE BILL'S RANCH
Located west on U.S. 64 at Blue Hawk Peak are Pawnee Bill's original mansion and several ranch buildings - with artifacts, furniture, clothing, weapons and art objects collected by Pawnee Bill - famous showman and partner of Buffalo Bill.

1. DEEP SEAPORT — TULSA
2. WILL ROGERS' SHRINE
3. BLACK MESA
4. PAWNEE BILL'S RANCH

OREGON

CAPITAL - **SALEM**

33rd. STATE
FEBRUARY 14, 1859

AREA -96,981 sq. miles
-251,181 sq. km.

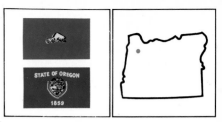

1

Nicknamed the "Beaver State", Oregon holds a wide variety of landscapes. The Cascade Range divides the state into two distinct climatic zones. Warm and moist sea winds create lush vegetation on the western side of the range, while the area to the east of these mountains is dry. Several other snow-clad peaks, including Mt. Jefferson and the Three Sisters, are almost as high. The rugged coastline has several natural harbors. Crater Lake was formed by the eruption and collapse of the prehistoric volcano Mount Mazama. With nearly one half of the land covered with forests, Oregon leads the nation in lumber production. Agriculture is also an important industry; and Portland ranks among the country's top wheat ports. With its scenic coastline, mountain ranges, high plateaus and 13 national forests Oregon offers a wide variety of recreational facilities.

The United States claimed Oregon in 1792, after Capt. Robert Gray's discovery of the Columbia River. Later, the Lewis and Clark expeditions aroused further interest in the region. Until the early 1840's, most of the Americans living in Oregon were trappers and missionaries. In August 1848 Oregon was organized as a territory —with Joseph Lane as the first territorial governor.

CRATER LAKE

Thousands of years ago Mount Mazama stood on the site of Crater Lake. After violent eruptions, the molten rock drained away the subterranean cracks and the 12,000-foot volcano collapsed, leaving a great depression which is now Crater Lake. The brilliant blue lake is 6 miles across and has a 20-mile shoreline, surrounded by lava cliffs that rise 500 to 2,000 feet above the water level.

BONNEVILLE LOCK AND DAM

The U.S. Army Corps of Engineers began construction here in 1933. The dam is located 145 miles from the mouth of the Columbia River, in the heart of the beautiful Cascade Range.

MT. HOOD 11,345'

The highest point in Oregon is famous for year round skiing at rustic Timberline Lodge and the Meadows. Geo-thermal heat from Mt. Hood promises to be a source of energy for Portland and the surrounding community.

THREE FINGERED JACK

Three Fingered Jack is located in the Mount Jefferson wilderness area. Rising to an elevation of 7,841 feet, it is part of the central portion of the Cascades. The Pacific Crest National Scenic Trail skirts its western slope — 7 miles north of the Santiam Pass off U.S. Highway 20.

MULTNOMAH FALLS

Rising 620 feet, Multnomah Falls is the second highest in the United States. Adjoining Benson State Park, the falls are located in the Columbia River Gorge, 30 miles east of Portland.

2

3

4

5

1. CRATER LAKE
2. BONNEVILLE LOCK AND DAM
3. HAYSTACK ROCK
4. THREE FINGERED JACK
5. MOUNT HOOD
6. MULTNOMAH FALLS

6

PENNSYLVANIA

CAPITAL -
HARRISBURG

2nd. STATE
DECEMBER 12, 1787

AREA -45,333 sq. miles
-117,412 sq. km.

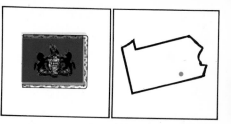

1

2

3

Pennsylvania is known as the "Keystone State" because of its tangible position among the 13 colonies. Its early leadership played an important role in the formation of our great nation. The drive for self-determination, which was clearly reflected in all the colonies, is documented forever in places like Philadelphia and Valley Forge. When the sound of the cannon boomed in 1861, Pennsylvania was ready to fight for freedom for all men on the side of the Union. In the great battle of. Gettysburg the challenge was won, and the Union was preserved.

Although the Civil War had a great effect on the nation, it was instrumental in stimulating the phenomenal growth of Pennsylvania into the industrial giant that it is today . . . rich in coal, and one of the leading producers of steel.

Located in the northeastern part of the country, Pennsylvania is a state of natural beauty. Its mountains, streams, lakes, and its famed Amish Pennsylvania Dutch community make it a popular place to visit.

GETTYSBURG
Gettysburg will be remembered in the hearts of men as being the scene of one the bloodiest battles of the Civil War. About 51,000 Union and Confederate soldiers lost their lives there. This decisive battle broke the strength of the Confederacy. President Lincoln delivered his famous Gettysburg Address there on November 19, 1863.

I-80 OVER ALLEGHENY RIVER — EMLENTON
Often called "Main Street U.S.A.", I-80 runs between New York City and San Francisco, and is the most direct route between these cities. This bridge is the highest bridge east of the Mississippi River.

INDEPENDENCE HALL — PHILADELPHIA
One of the country's most famous landmarks, this is the place where the Declaration of Independence was adopted on July 4, 1776; and where the Constitution of the United States was created in 1787.

1. GETTYSBURG
2. GETTYSBURG
3. I-80 OVER ALLEGHENY RIVER — EMLENTON
4. INDEPENDENCE HALL — PHILADELPHIA

4

RHODE ISLAND

CAPITAL -
PROVIDENCE
13th. STATE
MAY 29, 1790

AREA -1,214 sq. miles
-3,144 sq. km.

1

Rhode Island is the smallest state in the Union, but the official name, State of Rhode Island and Providence Plantations, is the longest name of any state. Rhode Island was the first of the original 13 colonies to declare her independence from Great Britain, but she was the last colony to ratify the Constitution. She did not ratify until 1790, when the Bill of Rights was ready to be added to the Constitution.

Rhode Island is an important industrial state, and ranks high in the production of jewelry and textiles. She supplies local markets with a variety of fruits and vegetables, and fishermen receive their livelihood from her abundant supply of seafood.

Rhode Island's location on the Narragansett Bay makes her a choice vacation spot. Sun worshipers flock to her beaches during the summer to enjoy boating, fishing and other water sports.

H.M.S. ROSE
On the waterfront at King's Dock, is the only Revolutionary War frigate afloat, and is the last full-rigged ship sailing on the east coast. The H.M.S. Rose was responsible for forming the U.S. Navy; and today visitors can view uniforms from the Colonial and Revolutionary era . . . as well as many different types of weapons.

THE BREAKERS
One of the many magnificent mansions located in Newport, the Breakers was built in 1895 for Cornelius Vanderbilt. Designed by Richard Morris Hunt, it resembles the northern Italian palaces of the 16th Century. The grounds overlook the Atlantic Ocean and Cliff Walk.

NEWPORT
Newport has something for every type of person. Noted for being "America's First Vacationland", she has many beach resorts; is the home of the American Cup Races; and is the birthplace for musical festivals featuring jazz, folk and opera. Newport displays many facets. Casual, formal or just relaxed, her atmosphere is never dull. Her many mansions give visitors a chance to experience the elegance of her historical past, and provide many hours of enjoyment.

FORT ADAMS
Originally intended to guard the entrance to Narragansett Bay, Fort Adams is one of the largest seacoast fortifications in the country. Visitors are provided with a visual record of the fort's military activities —from 1820 to the end of World War II. The location of the Naval Academy during the Civil War, her walls have housed many famous United States generals, such as Generals Burnside and Rosecrans; and Confederate Generals Braxton Bragg and John Magruder.

1. H.M.S. ROSE
2. THE BREAKERS
3. NARRAGANSETT PIER
4. FORT ADAMS

SOUTH CAROLINA

CAPITAL -
COLUMBIA

8th. STATE
MAY 23, 1788

AREA -31,055 sq. miles
-80,432 sq. km.

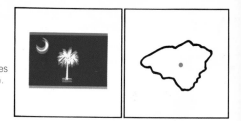

South Carolina is the epitome of the "New South". Before the Civil War it was totally agrarian; a land of sleepy cotton fields and widespread plantations. Since World War II, however, prosperity has supplanted lassitude, and South Carolina is presently a land of booming factories and energetic growth.

These drastic changes did not occur at the expense of the "Palmetto" state's traditional charm. Tourists may visit historic cities like Charleston, drive through rolling countryside marked with elegant plantations, and explore the shoreline of the historically-famous South Carolina coast.

KINGS MOUNTAIN — NATIONAL MILITARY PARK
The third largest military park in the United States, this park encompasses 3,950 acres of land, a battlefield ridge about 2 thousand feet long, and a narrow hogback 100 feet above the surrounding valleys.

FORT SUMTER-CHARLESTON
This declared national monument is a "must" on a sightseeing tour of the United States. The brick and stone fortification was built between 1829 and 1860. When the Federal troops in Fort Sumter were fired upon by the Confederate troops, it signaled the beginning of the Civil War.

HARTWELL DAM AND RESERVOIR
Located on the Savannah River, between Anderson, South Carolina and Hartwell, Georgia, the $100,000,000.00 dam is 240 feet high and impounds a reservoir of 60,000 acres —with a shoreline of 960 miles. The U.S. Highway 29 bridge is seen in the foreground. The area abounds with accommodations for fishing, boating and relaxing.

HARBOR TOWN — HILTON HEAD ISLAND
This fabulous new port of the Intracoastal Waterway looks like a flower from the air. Appearing very much like a Mediterranean village, Harbor Town is one of the attractions of Sea Pines Plantation. The "Tree Houses", or Sea Loft Villas, are located in upper portion of photograph.

1. KINGS MOUNTAIN — NATIONAL MILITARY PARK
2. FORT SUMTER — CHARLESTON
3. HARTWELL DAM AND RESERVOIR
4. HARBOR TOWN — HILTON HEAD ISLAND

SOUTH DAKOTA

CAPITAL - **PIERRE**

40th. STATE
NOVEMBER 2, 1889

AREA -77,047 sq. miles
-199,552 sq. km.

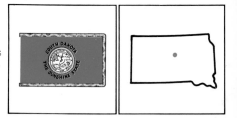

1

2

3

The Missouri River, flowing southward through the center of South Dakota, divides the state into 2 regions. To the east, the land is flat or gently rolling with some hills and many lakes. The western side holds beautiful grasslands and buttes in the northwest, and the Badlands and Black Hills in the southwest.

The economy is founded mainly on agriculture. A larger percentage of people make their living through agriculture in South Dakota than in any other state. The mines of the Black Hills, after nearly a century of continuous production, still yield millions of dollars each year. The largest working gold mine in the Western hemisphere is in Lead, South Dakota.

For many years the Indians have been central figures in South Dakota's history. The state's Indian population today is the largest in the country, with the Sioux being the most numerous. During the early years, fur trading was the principal activity. The Louisiana Purchase and the Lewis and Clark expeditions opened up the area to commerce. In 1831 the first steamboat on the Upper Missouri River gave easy accessibility to the Dakota fur trade.

In 1859 Yankton became the first capital of the Dakota territory. Further development was spurred by the railroad lines that came into Yankton in the 1870's. Gold was discovered in the Black Hills in 1874, but its source, contained in the sacred lands of the Indians, led to much bloodshed . . . culminating in the annihilation of Custer at the Battle of Little Big Horn. The Dakota territory was established in 1861, but due to irreconcilable differences, the territory was divided and admitted as North Dakota and South Dakota in 1889.

MOUNT RUSHMORE
Created by Gutzon Borglum, Mount Rushmore is one of the largest pieces of sculpture ever completed. The faces of Washington, Jefferson, Lincoln and Theodore Roosevelt, each 60 feet high, were carved with intricate perfection - 400 feet above the valley of the Black Hills. Special terraces and observation points are provided to allow a variety of places for viewing.

CORN PALACE-MITCHELL
Two to three thousand bushels of various shades of natural-colored corn and grain are used each year to decorate the Corn Palace. Designs formed from corn, and outlined with grains and grasses, are used to decorate both the exterior and interior of this structure. The Corn Palace Festival is held every year.

OAHE — PIERRE
Founded in 1880, Pierre was chosen as the state capital in 1890. Pierre gets its name from Fort Pierre, the former fur trading post across the Missouri River that was the state's first permanent white settlement. The Oahe Dam is nearby to the north and the city of Pierre is the site of the U.S. Indian School and Hospital.

BADLANDS
The area of about 111,529 acres, lying within Pennington and Jackson counties, is well known as Badlands National Monument. Established in 1938, this area contains some of the most spectacular examples of erosion and weathering in the world. Pinnacles of varying colors - alternating with grayish-white sediments - are interspersed among irregular ravines, beautiful ridges, low hills and cliffs.

4

5

1. MOUNT RUSHMORE — NEAR RAPID CITY
2. CORN PALACE — MITCHELL
3. PIERRE
4. HARNEY PEAK & NEEDLES (Elevation 7,242 ft.)
5. BADLANDS

TENNESSEE

CAPITAL -
NASHVILLE

16th. STATE
JUNE 1, 1796

AREA -42,244 sq. miles
-109,412 sq. km.

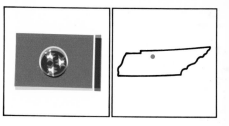

Tennessee emerged from the 19th Century with cotton fields ripening in the sun into the 20th Century with atomic energy at Oak Ridge.

Her mountains are majestic . . . the best known being the Great Smokies, with elevations of 6,643 feet at Clingmans Dome. Its numerous lakes and rivers play a major role in the state's economy.

Here, too, the famous Tennessee Walking Horses are raised. They are world-renowned for their graceful step in the show ring.

Nashville, home of the Grand Ole Opry and country music, is known throughout the world for its famous recording artists. It is referred to as the "recording capital" of the world.

Bristling and unique cities like Memphis, Knoxville and Chattanooga, have carefully preserved their heritage of the past while reflecting the "new" as well. They are a vital part of Tennessee's future.

NORRIS DAM
Located on the Clinch River, this dam provides electric power and flood control; and forms Norris Lake, a popular vacation area. It also provides the fertile valleys of the Appalachian Ridge with an ample reserve water supply.

CADES COVE — GREAT SMOKY MOUNTAINS NATIONAL PARK
An 11-mile loop road takes you back a hundred years... as you visit early settlers' cabins, beautiful waterfalls, and an operating Grist Mill at the Cable Farm in the lush green valley surrounded by the Great Smoky Mountains.

CLINGMANS DOME
Clingmans Dome rises 6,643 feet, and is the highest mountain in the Great Smoky Mountains National Park. An access road from Newfound Gap leads to an overlook parking area —where a paved footpath, a mile long leads to an observation tower on the summit.

NATCHEZ TRACE STATE PARK
This park encompasses 46,000 acres. The modern Natchez Trace Parkway, originally an Indian footpath, stretches from Nashville to Natchez, Mississippi. The park is about 95 % forest, and offers the visitor a full range of recreational opportunities.

FORT LOUDOUN DAM — LENOIR CITY
In this aerial view one can see the great magnitude of this dam. It has one of the world's highest single lift locks.

1. NORRIS DAM
2. CADES COVE — GREAT SMOKY MOUNTAINS NATIONAL PARK
3. CLINGMANS DOME
4. NATCHEZ TRACE STATE PARK
5. FORT LOUDOUN DAM — LENOIR CITY

3

4

5

TEXAS

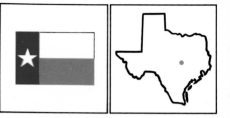

1

Texas, our second largest state, has a rich and colorful history, dating back to the Spanish Conquistadors of the 1500's. Today it is a blend of the old and new. The cowboy, with his ten-gallon hat and trusty quarter horse, still rides the vast plains; the oil wells still pump that precious "black gold", and cotton ripening into full bloom under the hot Texas sun, is still a major part of the state's economy.

But a New Frontier has also become an integral part of Texas. The Frontier of Space. Since the 1960's, beginning with Mission Control, Texas has become the permanent home of our astronauts.

Manufacturing is now the primary source of income in Texas. Chemical plants and other factories have taken over where once cattle and oil reigned supreme. The "Lone Star State" has a very diversified terrain and climatic changes that make many kinds of agriculture possible.

No matter which way you look at it —whether traveling by car, train or plane —Texas is huge! It represents

4 major geographic zones in its borders. From its highest elevations in the Guadalupe Mountains —to the awesome splendor of the Rio Grande and Pecos Rivers and its 624 miles of coastline, Texas is a spectacular state to live in and to visit.

ALAMO — SAN ANTONIO

The Alamo was a mission church, established by the Spanish in the early part of the 18th Century. The church structure, standing today in downtown San Antonio, was begun in 1755. The great drama the mission played occurred in 1836 —when a handful of defenders tried to defend the mission against the well-trained Mexican Army. Gallant men, like Davey Crockett, Jim Bowie and William Travis, fought fiercely and valiantly for 13 days. Although they lost their lives at the Alamo, their courage paved the path for Texan independence from Mexico.

JOHNSON SPACE CENTER

This huge complex, located 25 miles southeast of downtown Houston, was completed in September 1963, and covers an area of 1,620 acres. The Center's many responsibilities include getting the astronauts ready for manned space flights, and testing space craft equipment. Mission Control is the astronaut's link with earth from lift-off at Cape Kennedy in Florida to splashdown in the Pacific Ocean.

SAN JACINTO MONUMENT AND BATTLESHIP TEXAS — HOUSTON

This monument, which rises 570 feet above the coastal plain, commemorates the decisive battle in which Texas won its independence from Mexico in 1836. At the base of the monument is the San Jacinto Museum of Texas History. Also included in this state park is the Battleship Texas, presented to the state of Texas by the U.S. Navy. This battleship served in World War I as well as in World War II.

GUADALUPE PEAK

These mountains have elevations from 3,650 feet to 8.751 feet, and the Guadalupe Peak is the highest point in Texas. They are part of the Guadalupe Mountains National Park encompassing 77,518 acres.

1. ALAMO VILLAGE
2. JOHNSON SPACE CENTER
3. SAN JACINTO MONUMENT AND BATTLESHIP TEXAS — HOUSTON
4. ALAMO — SAN ANTONIO
5. GUADALUPE PEAK

2

4   3

5

UTAH

CAPITAL -
SALT LAKE CITY

45th. STATE
JANUARY 4, 1896

AREA -84,916 sq. miles
-219,932 sq. km.

1

Nicknamed the "Beehive State", Utah is well known for her inland sea and abundance of unusual geological structures. Her many national parks contain towering mountains, brightly-colored canyons, lush valleys and large salt and alkali deserts.

Utah is the resting place of the "Golden Spike", drive into the railroad tracks in 1869 to join the East and the West. Her oldest form of industry is farming, and it is her greatest source of wealth. Known for her mining and manufacturing, Utah supplies many different kinds of mineral ores to the rest of the United States.

Two Franciscan priests, Fathers Escalante and Dominguez, led the first expedition of white men ever to enter Utah in 1776. The Great Salt Lake was discovered in 1824 by James Bridger. And on July 24, 1847, Brigham Young, heading a group of Mormons, founded Salt Lake City. The state capital today, Salt Lake City is the home of the Mormon Tabernacle Choir.

In 1848 the Treaty of Guadalupe-Hidalgo ended the Mexican War and gave the Utah territory to the United States. The territory was established officially in 1850, with Brigham Young as governor. Statehood was granted in 1896.

ARCHES NATIONAL MONUMENT

Arches National Monument gets its name from all the erosion-carved openings in the vertical slabs of this red-rock country. The effects of weather have enlarged these openings to resemble arches. Within the 73,235 acres of park lies Landscape Arch, the longest natural stone span in the world —with a width of 291 feet and a height of 105 feet.

LAKE POWELL

Surrounded by Glen Canyon National Recreation Area, the lake is 180 miles long and is filled with trout and bass. The shoreline is longer than the entire United States west coast.

GOOSENECKS STATE PARK

Goosenecks State Park gives visitors a bird's-eye view of the "gooseneck" canyons of the San Juan River, which flows into Lake Powell 1,200 feet below.

ZION NATIONAL PARK

Zion National Park is located in Utah's spectacular desert and canyon country. Spreading 230 square miles, the park is the home of the splendid, multi-colored gorge known as Zion Canyon. Two gigantic stone masses form the southern entrance to the park —"The Watchmen" and "West Temple" — which rises 3,795 feet and is the most distinct formation in this section. The Kolob section is a region of rocks, some elevated more than 8,000 feet above sea level, and the home of the finger-like, red sandstone canyons. This area was once known as Zion National Monument.

BRYCE CANYON

Named for Ebenezer Bryce, a cattle grazer from this region, Bryce Canyon is 36,000 acres of some of the earth's most colorful rocks —shaped by years of erosion into unusual forms. Bowl-shaped amphitheatres of colorful cliffs and pinnacles were formed by the tributaries of the Paria River. Walls and spires, which occur in abundance, were shaped by the erosion of hard and soft layers of rock. The red, yellow and brown tints of the canyon are caused by traces of iron oxides; and in some places, manganese oxides lend a lavender hue.

2

1. ARCHES NATIONAL MONUMENT
2. LAKE POWELL
3. GOOSENECKS STATE PARK
4. ZION NATIONAL PARK
5. BRYCE CANYON

3

4

5

VERMONT

CAPITAL -
MONTPELIER
14th STATE
MARCH 4, 1791
AREA -9,609 sq. miles
-24,887 sq. km.

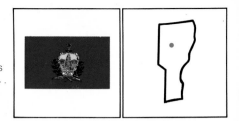

1

2

Vermont is the 2nd largest of the New England states, and her nickname is the "Green Mountain State". The Green Mountains are the backbone of Vermont, extending the length of the state into both Quebec and Massachusetts. They are part of the Appalachian Highlands —along with all the other land regions of Vermont. Over 65 % of the state is forested with many different varieties of trees. Vermont is known as an agricultural state, but industrial production and recreational industries have become most important in recent years.

Fort Dummer became the first permanent English community in 1724. With the help of the Indians, the French fought for control of Vermont from 1744 to 1759. They finally gave up their claim to Great Britain. Meanwhile, the governor of New-Hampshire claimed almost all of Vermont, and started to give pioneers permits to settle. New York protested, and tried to force the settlers to again purchase land from Albany. A local militia known as the Green Mountain Boys fought to protect the settlers, and after many successful battles, Vermont became an independent state. In 1791 Vermont became the 14th State of the Union, the first to be added to the original 13 colonies.

SHELBURNE MUSEUM

Shelburne Museum is an outdoor museum of early New England life. It has 35 buildings, some of which were moved there brick by brick, and restored to original condition. On the 45 acres of grounds are many 18th and 19th Century exhibits depicting the life and handiwork of the people from that era.

BARRE

The largest granite-producing district in the United States since 1900, Barre is frequently referred to as the granite center of the world. Many large plants are located in Barre for the making of memorials and monuments.

1. SHELBURNE MUSEUM   2. BARRE

VIRGINIA

CAPITAL -
RICHMOND

10th. STATE
JUNE 25, 1788

AREA -40,817 sq. miles
-105,716 sq. km.

Virginia is a state of history, spice and memorabilia. Vacationers may spend months uncovering the treasures that this state of "variety" has to offer.

The idea of preservation is obviously present in Virginia. Colonial Williamsburg, Jamestown and Yorktown, all connected by the Colonial Parkway, embody the core of American independence.

The tourist will find enjoyment in the beautiful mountains and along the glorious eastern shore. Virginia's beaches and seafood are reputed to be among the best on the eastern coast.

All who visit this enchanting state will be enthralled by the birthplaces and homes of George Washington, Thomas Jefferson, Robert E. Lee and others. They will better understand the present as they trace the echoes of the past in the extraordinary land of Virginia.

WILLIAMSBURG

Originally an outpost of Jamestown called "Middle Plantation", this area became a bustling center for the

colony due to its strategic location and the strength of its defenses. It was the capital of the colony for 80 years. Today it is called Williamsburg —in honor of King William III, who laid out the plans for the city. Colonial Williamsburg is a favorite site for visitors because of its historical value and quaint authenticity.

CHESAPEAKE BAY BRIDGE TUNNEL — NORFOLK

Extending over and under the Chesapeake Bay, this is one of the 7 engineering wonders of the world. Travelling by automobile on the Bay Bridge Tunnel (over 17 miles), you will see fascinating views of the Atlantic, the Bay, and the streams of warships and merchant vessels.

APPOMATTOX COURT HOUSE

The McLean home at Appomattox Court House was the scene of a great historical event. Confederate General Lee surrendered to Union General Grant after an unsuccessful attempt to break through the Union army's blockade. On this site they negotiated the terms that ended the Civil War. Somewhere in the Federal lines troops cheered. Grant ordered silence, saying "The Rebels are our countrymen again!"

1. WILLIAMSBURG
2. CHESAPEAKE BAY BRIDGE TUNNEL
3. MOUNT VERNON
4. APPOMATTOX COURT HOUSE

WASHINGTON

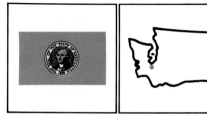

1

2

3

The only state named for a president, Washington is a gateway for land, sea and air travel to Alaska and Asia. The "Evergreen State" is so called for its many fir, hemlock, pine and other coniferous trees —making Washington a leading producer of lumber.

The state has over 3,000 miles of shoreline that makes it possible to export its lumber — as well as its beef, delicious apples, cherries, beans and other agricultural products. Famous for its fishing, Washington is especially noted for its Chinook and Sockeye salmon. Reports of early explorers tell of a rich fur trade in the northwest. The traders were followed by the missionaries. In 1836 Marcus Whitman and his wife established a mission near Walla Walla, which they ran for 11 years.

1. SEATTLE
2. GRAND COULEE DAM
3. MOUNT RAINIER
4. OLYMPIC NATIONAL PARK

Then in 1847 Indians massacred them —along with several of their fellow workers.

"Fifty Four Forty or Fight" was the slogan used during the presidential campaign of 1844, but the boundary between Washington and Canada was fixed at latitude 49 degrees by the 1846 Treaty of Oregon.

SEATTLE

"The hills of the greenest green are in Seattle." And Seattle is also famous for the Seattle Center —which harbored the 1962 Seattle World's Fair. At the Center, called the "people's place", one can find a constant medley of sport, cultural and recreational activities —as well as convention and restaurant facilities. A monorail whisks people from downtown Seattle to the Center. This 1.2 mile trip takes 90 seconds and costs only 10c. The highest point of the park is the 607-foot-tall Space Needle.

GRAND COULEE DAM

The construction of Grand Coulee Dam began in 1933 and was finished in 1941. It ranks as the mightiest piece of masonry ever built by man, comprising 10,585,000 cubic yards of concrete. The Grand Coulee provides tremendous electrical power, and its water irrigates the Columbian Basin —where farmers raise large crops of vegetables on land that was once dry and barren.

MOUNT RAINIER

The highest mountain in the state, Mt. Rainier is located southeast of Tacoma and Seattle. Its 14,410-foot elevation, and its large glaciers challenge many mountain climbers. Mount Rainier National Park is open all year round.

OLYMPIC NATIONAL PARK

This park is a 1,400-square-mile expanse of wild forest and glacier-studded mountains. At lower elevations one will find coniferous rain forests, lakes, streams and a 50-mile seacoast, with rocky headlands, beaches and a thriving wildlife population. Also found in the park are 60 glaciers . . . plus a jungle-like rain forest.

4

WEST VIRGINIA

CAPITAL -
CHARLESTON

35th. STATE
JUNE 20, 1863

AREA -24,181 sq. miles
-62,629 sq. km.

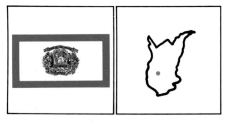

1

2

3

West Virginia, located in the Appalachian Highlands, is nicknamed the "Mountain State" because of her extreme ruggedness. The steep and rocky terrain of West Virginia makes farming an almost impossible task, but her large mineral deposits have made her a prominent industrial state —producing more coal than any other state in the union. Many of her industrial cities lie along the Ohio River, which forms the western border of the state. West Virginia's scenic mountains and mineral springs attract vacationers throughout the year.

Until the Civil War, West Virginia was part of Virginia, but her loyalty belonged to the Union, and she became a separate state in 1863. The state motto, "Mountaineers Are Always Free", states clearly the sense of independence that the people of West Virginia still feel today.

West Virginia is a songwriter's dream —where farm-dotted country roads lead to towns like Left Hand, Peel Tree or Wheeling. It is a composite of towering wooded mountains, deep valleys, and broad rolling plateaus. Sightseers enjoy an old-time logging train that runs a few miles from an important radio-telescopic observatory. The mountains provide vacationers with an inexpensive holiday, and are a camper's delight.

Built on coal and courage, West Virginia offers her splendid natural beauty to the nation.

WHITE SULPHUR SPRINGS

White Sulphur Springs is located 80 miles southeast of Charleston, the capital of West Virginia, and 4 miles from Virginia's border. One of the most luxurious resorts in the United States, the city's main attractions are mountain scenery and medicinal springs. Settled in 1774, the area was a well known resort by the 1830's. The Old White, a famous hotel, was used as a hospital during the Civil War. Standing in its place today is the Greenbrier Hotel, a noted spa since the mid-19th century.

HARPERS FERRY

Harpers Ferry is located in a gap of the Blue Ridge Mountains where the Potomac and Shenandoah Rivers merge. Its scenic location was described by Thomas Jefferson as "one of the most stupendous scenes in nature". Robert Harper purchased the site of the city in 1748 and built a ferry across the Potomac River. The city is the site of the Harper's Ferry National Monument —which consists of the arsenal seized on October 16, 1859 by John Brown and his followers during the Civil War. Because of her position in the Shenandoah Valley, and her railroad facilities, Harpers Ferry was a strategic base throughout the Civil War. Several thousand Union troops surrendered here to the Confederates under Stonewall Jackson in 1862.

PINNACLE ROCK — BLUEFIELD

Pinnacle Rock, which resembles the ruins of an ancient temple, stands as a tall and slender monument of quartzite sandstone 2,700 feet above sea level. The park has a 15-acre lake formed by an earthen dam and filled from mountain streams. Trails lead to vantage points around the rock where visitors can overlook many mountain ridges.

MOUNDSVILLE

Moundsville is located on the Ohio River at the mouth of Little Grave Creek. Settled in 1774, she takes her name from the Grave Creek Mound, one of the largest Indian burial mounds in the country.

1. WHITE SULPHUR SPRINGS
2. HARPERS FERRY
3. PINNACLE ROCK — BLUEFIELD
4. I-77 TUNNELING UNDER APPALACHIAN TRAIL
5. MOUNDSVILLE

4

5

WISCONSIN

CAPITAL -
MADISON

30th. STATE
MAY 29, 1848

AREA -56,154 sq. miles
-145,439 sq. km.

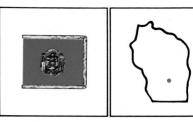

1

Wisconsin, bordered by Lake Superior on the north and Lake Michigan on the east, is nicknamed the "Badger State", and is sometimes referred to as "America's Dairyland".

The first white man to explore the Wisconsin Territory back in 1634 was Jean Nicolet, a Frenchman. France established a good rapport with the Indians, and a lucrative fur trade resulted. War broke out in 1712 between France and the Fox Indians for control of the Fox and Wisconsin Rivers. The final outcome weakened France's position with the Indians. The French were there until 1763; the British until 1783. Then, by the Ordinance of 1787, the Wisconsin country became part of the Northwest Territory.

Today Wisconsin is one of the most progressive states —having made many political, economic and social changes since the 1900's. Many of these reforms were later adopted by other states and the United States government. The Republican Party was founded there in 1854.

Wisconsin has long been famous for its dairy products, and beautiful farms in the rolling green countryside. But today manufacturing takes precedence over dairying, and is the chief source of income for the state.

The natural beauty of Wisconsin lures millions of vacationers every year to sample its vast recreational opportunities. The state is sometimes referred to as "God's Country" . . . an appropriate name for such beauty and versatility.

MITCHELL OBSERVATORY — MILWAUKEE
One of the most interesting horticultural gardens in the country is located in Milwaukee. At the Mitchell Observatory visitors can see plants growing in their natural environments, whether arid or jungle.

VILLA LOUISE — PRAIRIE DU CHIEN
This villa is located in Prairie du Chien, onetime military post and center of John Jacob Astor's fur empire.

WISCONSIN DELLS
The Wisconsin Dells pass through 4 counties of the state and are one of Wisconsin's most beautiful areas. Over many years the Wisconsin River has cut a channel seven miles long and 100 feet deep . . . through layers of soft sandstone. Many unusual formations have been carved out of the rock, and they bear strange names like: Grand Pisno, Devil's Elbow and Fat Man's Misery.

1. MITCHELL OBSERVATORY — MILWAUKEE
2. VILLA LOUISE — PRAIRIE DU CHIEN
3. A DAIRY FARM IN THE DAIRY STATE
4. WISCONSIN DELLS

2

3

4

WYOMING

CAPITAL -
CHEYENNE

44th. STATE
JULY 10, 1890

AREA -97,914 sq. miles
-253,597 sq. km.

Wyoming has all the ingredients of a super-classic Western movie —with its beautiful scenic mountains, vast rangeland, Indians, trappers, oilmen and cowboys . . riding off into the sunset on their trusty horses.

A popular tourist state, it is the home of the largest and oldest national park in the United States, the Yellowstone National Park —which attracts millions of visitors annually. Equally popular is the Grand Teton National Park, with its sharp peaks rising up from the landscape that teems with wildlife and scenic beauty.

Much of Wyoming's wealth lies in its cattle and oil. When the South Pass was discovered in 1824 it became a direct route through the mountains, and thousands of pioneers used it on their trek westward. Three of the old pioneer trails that crossed Wyoming were the Mormon, California and Oregon. Travellers from around the world use these same trails today — which have become interstate highways.

Wyoming is known as the "equality state", because it was the first in our nation to allow its women to vote.

OLD FAITHFUL

Yellowstone, our first national park, is the home of the most famous geyser in the world. Erupting within 45 to 85 minutes, with predictable regularity, to a height of 184 feet, Old Faithful graphically demonstrates the untapped sources of energy buried beneath the earth's surface.

GRAND TETONS

Located in the northwest section of Wyoming, the Grand Tetons are awesome to behold, with their sharp peaks rising up from a beautiful valley floor called Jackson Hole. They range in height to 13,770 feet.

DEVILS TOWER

Composed of volcanic igneous rock, the 865-foot Devils Tower was our first national monument. Once a landmark for pioneers, more than 2,000 people have climbed Devils Tower. However, the most dramatic ascent was in 1941, when a parachutist jumped to the top of Devils Tower and was stranded for 6 days.

LOWER FALLS OF THE YELLOWSTONE RIVER

Plunging 308 feet, twice the height of Niagara Falls, spectacular Lower Falls is a favorite of artists and visitors alike. The green color comes from algae and moss growing on the rocks of the river bed. Combining the yellow rocks, the white water of the falls and the blue sky, nature has blended together an unsurmountable setting.

1. OLD FAITHFUL
2. GRAND TETONS
3. DEVILS TOWER
4. LOWER FALLS OF THE YELLOWSTONE RIVER

FRONT COVER PHOTO:
Golden Gate Bridge, California.

BACK COVER PHOTOGRAPHS:
Golden Gate Bridge, California. Statue of Liberty, New York.
Grand Canyon, Arizona. Miami Beach, Florida.
Haleakala National Park, Hawaii. Portage Glacier, Alaska.

Printed in Spain  GEOCOLOR®

Impreso en IGOL. Industria gráfica BARCELONA · D.L. B-22.040-19